WHEN I WAS A
BOY

A Personal History

JERRY THOMAS CAPLINGER

CONTENTS

CHAPTER ONE
THE EARLY YEARS

I'm told I was born in Hope, Arkansas on August 23, 1943, at 2:37 AM, that makes me a Leo, to anyone who follows astrology (but just barely so). The family was there because my daddy had a job working at the ammunition proving ground that was active there during the Second World War. I have no idea of the job that he performed, but I was told that he rode a bus daily with other workers to where their jobs were performed. I'm also told that, on the bus one day, one of the workers seated next to him began teasing a woman seated in front of them and that woman took a swing at him with a large handbag she was carrying. She missed the worker but hit my daddy on the head with whatever object she had inside, this caused him to have headaches for a long time afterwards.

I'm also told that I was small with a low birthweight and had to be placed in an incubator for a time. I suspect I was close to not making it through those first days. My mother said I was the easiest delivery of her six children, which is easily understandable given my size and weight. I was the second child, with an older brother who was close to being exactly two years older than me, with him having been born on August 1, 1941.

My earliest memory was being outside on the south side of our home in a flower garden area being bathed in the sun during the late morning hours on a very warm day.

That home, located near a community called "Shinewell," in rural southeastern Oklahoma (McCurtain County) was typical of those in that part of the country at that time. It was unpainted, plain on the inside and had outdoor facilities. It was situated near some tall pine trees on its west side that were beautiful trees and provided a lot of shade during the afternoons. A dirt road led from the house, on the north side, and turned east, out across the pasture to a gate. The county road that lay there, really, was just a cleared right-of-way for an unconstructed road through the forest. It was no better than the road through the pasture and had wet spots where natural water drainage seeped across. That left an area which turned into mud with any amount of rainfall, especially during the winter, spring, and early summer. Vehicles (typically Model-A Fords) would not take the same path through the wet areas to avoid making deep ruts through the bog. Those ruts could cause a vehicle to become stuck because of being "high-centered:" that is the bottom of the vehicle would be contacting the ground and the wheels could only spin due to losing traction.

The home and the 80 acres of land had been secured by my grandpa. He had bought it for back taxes from the local county government. Story is, that another man was intending to buy the land, but when the property came up for auction, he was gone getting a drink, so the sale proceeded with only one bidder. Per my mother, when the man returned, he became very upset, and when an additional parcel of land, which adjoined my grandpa's land, came up for auction, he bid against my grandpa just to drive up the price, which ended up at about $100. In this post-depression era, that was a lot of money.

My daddy had joined the Navy and was off in training in Mississippi, later serving as a quartermaster on a minesweeper in the Alaskan Aleutian Islands, while the family, along with my maternal grandmother, "Zona," lived on the acreage out among the trees. It is unclear whether he was drafted and didn't seek a deferment he could have gotten because of his family, or voluntarily entered the Navy. I suspect there was some tension in the home at that time.

This was a time of rationing for basic supplies like sugar and washing powder. I'm told that I took the precious washing powder and proceeded to pour it into a mud puddle in the dirt road near the home. My grandmother wasn't at all happy when she found out what I had done. Luckily, I don't remember. My mother told me that she was left with a Model A Ford that wasn't in the best of condition, in fact, the transmission became inoperable. Having no other resources, she unbolted the cover, sorted through what she had found, realigning some things, and got it working again. Later she took it for an oil change, but the worker failed to fill the crankcase with new oil; on the way home, the engine seized up making the car inoperable. I don't know what she did then.

When my daddy left for the war (I'll use the term "daddy," because that was what we called him) I was a baby. When he returned, per my mother, I was a little boy and much different in my behavior. I would have, most likely, regarded my daddy with a bit of standoffishness and felt he was, in many ways, a stranger. I really don't remember any of this.

The family then moved to a very small town in Polk County, Arkansas named Vandervoort. The town was named in honor of one of the developers of the Kansas City Southern Railroad. Incidentally, there was a system for picking up the mail bag from the town that strung the mail bag between two arms of a post near the railroad. When the train mail car came by, the bag was snagged by a mechanism on the car then subsequently retrieved inside the car. I thought that system (at a small age) to be ingenious.

My daddy's family lived in this small town, which was a principal reason for moving there. My grandfather helped my daddy get a job at a local sawmill. We lived in a rented house near the railroad, with another house between us and the railroad. I remember much of this, and I partially remember going over to the house next door, going up the steps and then going inside. I'm told I did this so much it was almost like I was living there. My mother, later, told me that I was cute, and the neighbors didn't seem to mind. My mother tried to stop me by telling me not to go there, but I ignored her and kept going. Finally, she resorted to putting me in an outbuilding (shed) and turning the latch on the outside, thus locking me inside. It was a shock to me to be locked inside with no way out (I still don't want to be in small places today - elevators especially). I got the message and no longer went visiting next door.

We next moved into a small house on the outskirts of this small (very) town. The house was located close to a bend in the graveled main road leading south, then running west out to the main north-south blacktop (sealed coating) highway (U.S. 71) that ran through the area. The house was small, had no electricity (I'm not sure that much of the town had electricity at that time either); it was situated across a dirt street from a low-lying creek bottom area. The creek lay between the home and the main part of the town, with the railroad essentially separating the creek area and our home from the main part of the town. The creek ran east to west in front of our house and was fed from the drainage of a large railroad water supply pond whose "Hoover Dam" like concave concrete shape was amazing to me and not far away from the house.

The water from the pond was clean, flowing amply and helped to provide a vast play area for my older brother and me. In later times, when I was a little older, my brother and I, at his instigation, used poles to vault the creek. We would run towards the creek with poles in hand, plant the poles in the creek bottom and ride its arc to the other side. That was much like competitive pole-vaulters do today, but we weren't looking to clear any high obstacle; we just wanted to make it to the other side of the creek without getting wet. At times, in the summer, we would play in the waters of the creek where it was wider and had a sandy bottom. I vividly remember black bugs that would run across the surface of the water, apparently (I know now) they were being supported by the surface tension of the water.

We used kerosene lamps to light the home and had a battery-powered radio. The lamps cast a soft glow that I really liked. We had one that was a floor lamp with a tall cylinder-like globe. I thought it was very nice with its ivory-colored base and accompanying shade. It gave me a special feeling to be near it when lit at night. The large radio (superheterodyne?), with its wooden case, sat on a trestle table that seemed specially made for this radio/battery arrangement. The radio battery was a large, packaged arrangement, of about 36-48, or more, D-cell (like) batteries. The outer battery container was brightly colored with yellow and black markings, as I best remember. The radio table was positioned near an east window. That radio and table would play an interesting role in a future event.

Mom cooked on a kerosene-fueled kitchen stove, and we had a real "ice box" requiring a large block of ice for a refrigerator. I remember Mom cooking my brother and me fried eggs for breakfast and serving them with slices of tomato; I still like that combination today.

Outside the home in the back was an oak tree with a limb that was at the right height for two swings. My brother and I would ride the swings and imagine we were like railroad trains starting from a standstill and building speed as we pumped the swings into higher, and higher, arcs.

My mom got her first washing machine during our time there, previously she only had a scrub board. The machine was powered by a small gasoline engine mounted under the main tub. The exhaust was run through a flexible steel tube to a small box-like muffler. The exhaust, however, was not far from the machine and the fumes it generated, which were smelly and unpleasant.

Outside the home, after we had lived there for a while, near the gravel road, a pile of small and short pine logs was deposited by someone unknown to me. These logs would eventually become fence posts by (I now know), being treated with a preservative (creosote), but before that could happen, the bark had to be removed and that was done by stripping it off with a drawer knife. It was a manual process that required the knife to be repeatedly drawn under the bark all the way around and over the entire length of the prospective posts. This was a piecework project that could result in a few dollars being brought into the family home. My brother and I were out there one day, I was about three years old at the time. My daddy suddenly appeared wearing a tiger face mask that had come on the back of a cereal box (Wheaties, probably). His appearance scared me, and I began to cry. His reaction was to scold me for being afraid. That scolding left me with a bad feeling, in addition to the fright, that I can still remember today.

Other times were not so bad: on a summer day my mother made lemonade using the big glass jar of a butter churn. We took the lemonade and rode in our old Chevrolet pickup following the gravel road out to and across the blacktop highway to the upper waters of the Rolling Fork River. The spot where we stopped was a shallow rocky pool where my brother and I found a long 2-inch by 12-inch board that we could ride through the water. We did that for some time that day which, obviously, has left a good and pleasant memory with me.

On some occasions, my brother and I were allowed to go to the sawmill where my daddy worked when it was not in operation. I remember seeing, from below the main deck and amid the sawdust, the mechanisms that enabled the mill to run and I seemed to understand a lot about how it all operated. There were long foot-wide belts connecting pulleys, these enabled the transfer of power between the various elements, and it all made some sort of sense to me. One time we were there in the early evening as a large flatbed trailer was being loaded with smoothly planed lumber by my daddy and others. Given current government regulations, my brother and I would never have been allowed anywhere close to the sawmill operations.

During the winter, my mom became due from her pregnancy; I was never aware of that. She was taken to the hospital in Mena, the county seat of Polk County, Arkansas. My brother and I were left with a neighbor couple who lived just up the road to the east of our house in what I remember to be a red brick home. I remember being served breakfast with fried eggs; I've always liked eggs and still do, to this day. When she came home, the baby was kept in bed with my mother, as we didn't have a crib, or a separate bed. I guess this was the same for me and my older brother when we were babies. There was another son born before a crib was procured. That was for my sister, who is seven years younger than I am. I seem to remember that this baby, my next younger brother, fell off the bed and may have injured his head. That may, partially, explain some issues he had later.

During our time at that home, the time came for it to be wired for electricity. The installer ran a ladder up into an opening in the outside wall above the living room. The ceilings for the whole house were merely paper that was supported by a lattice of crossed supports with open spaces between the supports. The electrician went up the ladder and I went right behind him. After entering the attic, I promptly lost my balance and fell, ripping through the paper ceiling and crashing into the living room. Luckily, or maybe not, I struck a corner of the trellis table holding the radio, which helped to break my fall. I don't remember being hurt, or crying, but my mother appeared nearby, from the kitchen, with an utterly bewildered look on her face.

At another time, my brother and I accompanied my daddy and another man to an area east of the town and, seemingly, further up the road that passed our house. I remember a partial clearing in the forest that served as a cemetery. My daddy and the other man proceeded to dig a grave. I noted that the sides of the grave and the corners were sharply defined, not like anything a backhoe would dig today. The corners, sides, and squareness of the grave would have enabled a rectangular solid shape to fit in it very well, and it was certainly deep enough to properly bury a casket.

My brother must have had a birthday, because there was a picture, I saw many times later, of him holding a brand-new BB rifle while standing beside a large white coconut cake. He must have been about six years old at the time and about ready to start school. This seems to have been the start of a pattern repeated several times in the future.

Grandparents' Home

Somewhere along during this time, I believe I was about 4, my older brother and I were permitted to go and spend a week, separately, with my mother's parents in deep southeastern Oklahoma. The home was in the same county area as Shinewell and near a place called "Goodwater." There must have been a reason for that name, and it must have been given by early settlers in the area. This had been my mother's home when she came to the area with her family during the end of the Great Depression years and was located about a half mile off the main gravel road that ran through the area. The road to the home was cut through the woods and had only bare earth for a surface.

My mother was an early teenager when the move into the home occurred; she shared many stories with me about her life at that time. It was hard to live, hard to go to school and the family had little money. Word is that my father was the first person she saw when she arrived at the Hayworth, Oklahoma school. I learned recently that my father had befriended her and that led to them later being married. She told me, in her later years, she didn't know what it was about her that "turned his head." Daddy once commented: "The first time I saw your mother."

The grandparents' home was built with a tin roof and no ceiling: that was nice during rain and thunderstorms. I remember an easy chair that had a metal frame with part of it sticking out of the arm, but that was no matter to me. That home was also wired for electricity due to the Rural Electrification Program from the government. The only electrical appliance in the home was a clock placed high up on a kitchen wall. My grandmother had a Singer sewing machine that was powered by a foot treadle. My mother later inherited that machine, replaced the machine with an electric one, but utilized the same cabinet until she stopped sewing.

When it came time for my parents to leave my grandparents' home, leaving me there, I was out by the wood pile using a hatchet to split some firewood for the kitchen stove.

During my visit, it became necessary for my grandmother to go to a small store to purchase some food supplies. A horse was saddled, and I was placed in the saddle. My grandmother then led the horse walking on foot through backwoods trails on a hot and humid summer day, opening several gates for what had to be two, or three, miles to reach the store. Then it was back across the same trail to return home.

An event involving my grandpa happened that I still don't understand. I followed him out into his barn and as we entered, he said: "You don't want to be no Mama's boy." I was only about three years old at the time and I was certainly "taken aback" (I now know that's descriptive of my reaction). Nothing else like that was ever said.

One day, at evening time, a flatbed truck arrived, and my grandmother and I boarded the open and side less bed of the truck, joining some others, for a ride to attend a religious tent revival in the Oklahoma – Arkansas border town of Cerrogordo. At the revival site, an olive drab colored tent had been set up, lighted by strings of bare yellow light bulbs. The yellow light bulbs were meant to not attract any flying insects, which would have been drawn to regular white light bulbs. Don't remember much about the service, but in my mind, I associate it with some "healing" activities popular at that time with other evangelists.

At another time, my grandmother and I attended another "evangelist" meeting in a church southwest of their home: I have no recollection of how we got there. There were three men in suits holding the service; one, I remember, had a baton, like a musical conductor's baton, only this one had alternating stripes (rings) down its length. I don't suspect that whatever "offering" these men collected was very substantial.

My grandmother grew a vine near the house which yielded gourds, these are plants which have bulbous-looking fruit about 6–8 inches long and 3-4 inches in diameter (there may have been some that were larger). The fruit, when dried, formed thick hardened shells which could be cut into shapes and utilized for many purposes. The one I remembered was cut in the form of a "dipper" and was used for dipping drinking water. This was a common practice in the area at that time.

A Family Move

My older brother started school in Vandervoort and was quickly promoted to the second grade, that was because he, apparently, could already read. Where, and how he learned that I don't know.

The family left Vandervoort shortly thereafter when my uncle Jack (my mother's sister's husband) helped my daddy get a job at the Dierks Forest Inc. treating plant in De Queen, AR. The was a good step up for the family, although I think my daddy was paid less than a dollar an hour, but that was good money at that time. He was given a job in the "operating room" where he controlled all the processes for filling the long "cylinders" with all the oil and chemicals that would saturate all the future utility poles and fence posts that were loaded into the cylinders; steam was then introduced to heat and pressurize the contents of the cylinders, thusly producing creosote treated utility poles and posts. Prior to treating, the cylinders were sealed by closing a very large circular door on the end using a ring of very large bolts. Occasionally, the cylinders had to be cleaned of debris which came off the poles during the treating process. This necessitated workers, including my daddy, entering the cylinders to their full depth to gather and clear the debris. The air in the cylinders had to be filled with the fumes of the oil and creosote. There was no OSHA regulation during those days.

Upon entering school in De Queen, my older brother was reassigned back to the 1st grade. To attend school, he rode in an old school bus that had substantial wire screens over the windows. There may have been good reasons for those screens, but they could have been an egress safety hazard and were not present on the school buses we later rode.

The new home we moved into was a farmhouse on some acreage several miles out, and to the east of, the town of De Queen. De Queen is the county seat of Sevier County, Arkansas. The home was situated off a gravel highway that led from De Queen to the next town named Lockesburg. That road (now Hwy 329) crossed over the Cossatot River (locally called "Cosstock") about five miles away, on an old iron bridge, which was typical of bridges in use at that time. The bridge had cross-planking providing linkage across the bridge frames and a smoother surface of "runners" for the vehicle's direction of travel.

The house itself was situated on the northeast side of a road corner, on the apex of a hill, with the gravel road making a curve to the right and descending to a small concrete bridge. This bridge crossed a small stream (creek) and that will be significant later in this story.

To the northwest of the house was a fenced cow lot and an old barn. The loft of the barn held a large amount of loose hay, which, I'm sure, had to have been gathered using pitchforks and, with great effort, placed in the barn. One wonders why the hay was unused and abandoned. There were acres of fields and woods that lay to the west of the barn; this area was used as pastureland later by our small herd of cows.

A dirt road to other homes/farms in the area came off the main road at the start of the curve and came through the barnyard, passing by the backside of the barn. A gate had to be opened for the cars to come through the barnyard area. My older brother and I began running out and opening the gate for cars that came through. We were doing that just to be helpful, but the drivers soon began tipping us with a penny, or two, or a nickel for our help. My daddy found out about us doing that and told us to stop taking these tips. I didn't think that was right at the time and, although the pattern of living among rural neighbors at that time was to generally help neighbors for free, I still don't agree with his directive.

The house on the place was built in a pattern often used in this rural area prior to the pre-WWII years. The kitchen and living room were together on the right side, with a bedroom to the left, but separating the two was an open corridor between the bedroom and the rest of the house. The kitchen had the cook stove for a heat source in winter, and the living room had a fireplace, but the bedroom had no heat at all.

The bedroom had two beds, one for my mother and daddy and the other for my brother and me. The younger brother, born prior to the move, would had to have still been kept on the bed with my parents. It also turned out, during that time, there was another baby brother born. I have no idea how that was accommodated in the home.

There was another problem with the bedroom: apparently there was a wasp nest, black ones, between the inside and outside walls by a window at the head of the bed. During the nights, several times a wasp came down and stung me and my brother. My daddy got some chewing tobacco, chewed it into a poultice, and applied it to the stings to ease the pain. I don't recall that it worked very well, but I guess that the thought of a pain reliever being applied helped as much as anything.

My brother and I had a wonderful playground on and around this land. Across the road from the front of the house lay a slightly wooded area that sloped down to a creek. Cows must have been kept in the area because the low tree leaves, and the brush were trimmed in the way that cattle do in a wooded area. The creek curved through the area, and we certainly found our way to it. In fact, we followed it to the bridge under the gravel road, and there, under the bridge, we caught large crawfish (crawdads, we called them) with our hands. We had to avoid their large pincers as we were doing this. We didn't see any snakes that I recall.

We had a milk cow, named "Old Beaut." She was black and white and must have been some derivative of a Holstein; she had a large milk bag and, apparently, gave sufficient milk to the family. She wore a large strap around her neck, which had a cowbell hung from it. Bells were used to locate the herd in a wooded area. Cows, typically, stay together out in the fields and woods. At one time, one heifer (a young cow which has not had a calf) got her head caught in a gulley between the roots of a tree and the gulley wall which was red dirt. The heifer bawled in panic and eventually was heard and freed by my daddy; he said the heifer sounded like a camel. My brother and I, of course, accompanied daddy as he did this, and I vividly recall the gulley and the tree root.

The Garden

The land behind the House was suitable for a garden and my daddy apparently decided to plant it, but some tools were needed to make this happen. One morning we got up early and were dressed for the cold air. I remember wearing a sweater and feeling the arms of it in the dim interior dash light of the old truck. In that old Chevrolet pickup truck, we headed to Texarkana, which lay about 50 miles to our south. We went to a Sears store where a "David Bradley" garden tractor was found and purchased, along with all its attachments: a turning plow, a harrow, a row cultivator, and a sickle bar mower. The machine had two large, automobile-sized drive wheels, a small gasoline engine, a large gear-reduction transmission and two handles for walk-behind steering and control. As daddy was pushing it toward the pickup to load it in the bed, the ratchets in the drive train were clicking, he said, amusedly, "listen to how it sounds."

The tractor was used to plow and plant a large garden that had many varieties of vegetables, watermelons, and rows of corn, which seemed very tall to me as a young child. I particularly remember some "Butterbeans" in an area on the garden's east side that grew in large yellow pods. I also remember helping my mother plant watermelon seeds in finger holes punched into small flat-topped earth mounds and then covering the seeds with dirt. A separate patch of ground further away from the house was tilled and planted in more corn. The area there was "new ground" and the stalks there were exceedingly tall in my perception as a young boy.

A young pig was kept in a rectangular pen between the barn and the garden. The pig rooted around in the ground creating large depressions in the soil. The pen was moved often to provide new areas for it to root and cleaner soil. This pig would come to an unforeseen end later.

The closest house to ours was about a quarter mile away to the west. It was the home of two ladies, one of whom had a boy with Downs Syndrome. He was a few years older than my brother and me, and we knew he was "different," but that made no difference to us. He wasn't, in any way, threatening us and seemed to enjoy our company. The home had a large Victrola style record player with its large horn-like speaker. We cranked it up and played it often. Later, the two women, who had no automobile, hitched up a team of horses to a wagon and drove off towards the small town of De Queen. I thought that was a very slow way to travel and it must have taken a full day for them to make the trip.

Mount Pleasant Church

While we lived in this area, the family began attending a small church in the Mount Pleasant Community. It was at this church, during Christmas Time, that I first heard the strands of "Silent

Night;" I thought its' sounds were extremely beautiful and magical in their effect.

That church was the beginning of my experience with religion, some of it for good and some of it less so, but it was also the beginning of religion's effect on the family in a major way. My daddy, at this time, was converted, convinced, accepted, or whatever is the proper term, and became a Christian. He stood, as was the custom I guess (I've never seen anything like this since) before the assembled congregation and told of his past. I remember him saying "I have taken the Lord's name in vain."

All of this led to him, and my mother, being baptized. I did not know what that meant and thought that my brother and I would have to go live with our grandparents, who were at that time, living near Broken Bow, Oklahoma. I asked my brother about this and found out that my fears weren't true. I was greatly relieved. The baptism took place in the Cossatot River near the bridge I described earlier. I remember them each wading out to about waist deep in the greenish and semi-clear river water where the preacher stood waiting. After having a handkerchief placed over their nose and mouth, and after hearing the words "I baptize you in the name of The Father, The Son, and The Holy Ghost'" they were each dunked backwards until they were fully under the water, then they were returned upright.

Later we attended a "Vacation Bible School" there and I remember getting gold and blue stars pasted on a record kept for the event; I think I did very well. On other occasions, there were joint dinners on the grounds; long tables were covered with cloth and the home-cooked dishes, provided by the ladies, were spread along their length. At times there were also "Singings" there and much of the afternoon was spent singing hymns. These were major occasions for these, and other, communities and townspeople.

The church was a multifunctional center for the community. At one time, a cooking demonstration, sponsored by the local electric power company (Southwestern Electric Power (later SWEPCO)), was conducted in the church by an attractive young woman using a new electric cooking range. The company had run the 220-volt electric power lines into the church specifically for this demonstration. The young woman was dressed in a business style much different from the common attire of the local ladies. Several dishes were cooked for the audience. In the meantime, my mother was still cooking on the kerosene stove that she had always had.

The New Chevy Pickup

After some time in this home, a brand new shiny black 1949 Chevrolet pickup truck was purchased; this turned out to be the only new vehicle purchased by the family. We used that new pickup to drive to Vandervoort for some purpose I'm not sure of. I think it was to pick up some household goods that needed to be brought to our new home. As we were on the return trip and while driving through a sub-mountainous area on Highway 71, the left rear wheel fell off the pickup. The axel dropped onto the pavement leaving a deep scratch in it and exposing the red clay subsurface layer below the thin blacktop.

The cause of the lost tire was untightened lug nuts under the hubcap that would never be detected without purposely removing the hubcap for an inspection, something that shouldn't need to be done on a new vehicle. The loose lug nuts allowed the edges of the rim holes to, over time, become enlarged until a failure occurred, which happened suddenly on that afternoon.

The tire rim was replaced, and the old one was left in the truck parking area close to some trees. The edge of the rim had a jagged place in it with a shard sticking out at an angle beyond the rim, but it seemed to be a plaything for me and my brother. As I was rolling the rim between my legs, the jagged portion came up and snagged the skin between my legs leaving a sizeable gash and exposing the yellow fat that had been under the skin in that area. Luckily, it wasn't a serious injury, and I don't remember any trouble with the healing process.

Playtime

The area we played in was mainly the road area between the gravel road and the gate by the barn, and thereabouts. In a sandy area we would pile the semi-wet sand over one foot, pack it down, then carefully remove the foot from the mound. The cavity that remained we called a "frog house" for toad frogs. I don't know if any frog ever visited one of our "houses," but we built these frequently.

At another time, in the summer and during the early evening, my brother and I were playing and running around the house. In the back yard and in a grassy area between the house and an outbuilding, called a shed, lay a multi-tined farm tool called a seedfork. This tool was like a pitchfork, but was wider and had many more tines, these were about an inch apart. The tines were curved so that, when in use, the they would aid in drawing materials toward the user. This seedford was lying in the grass with the tips of the tines in the air a few inches above the grass and faced in a direction that was directly into the clockwise circular path my brother and I were taking around the house. I noted this and, for whatever reason, I took a wider path on my next trip around the house. Sure enough, I ran into the fork and one of the tines penetrated my lower leg above the ankle. I was taken to the concrete platform that formed our back porch and I saw the dark blood run out of my leg onto the concrete. I was taken to the hospital in De Queen where an X-Ray was done (a first for me) and, after bandaging, was taken home.

Other Notable Events

During my brother's school year, he somehow started in the Cub Scouts; he was given a new Cub scout shirt with its colorful patches and its bandana. Later, on his birthday, he was given a new bicycle. This was a full-sized bike and much too big for me, but I, nevertheless, hopped on it and had to alternate sides of the frame between the seat and the front to reach the pedals, but I did that well enough, and I rode that bike, probably at age 5.

Along and about this time, I noticed that my right testicle had become larger than the left. I was taken to the health clinic by my daddy; he and the doctor talked about my condition, which was a hydrocele: a leakage of fluid from the abdomen into the scrotum through a small opening. The doctor talked about surgery to reverse something, but I, of course, didn't understand much of the conversation. This was not a serious condition and seemed to have corrected itself over time but did require some care not to compress the area. However, I was left with an imperfect body condition that remained for some time.

During this time, I also contracted "Pink Eye" (conjunctivitis) and was taken for treatment. It was recommended that the eyes be protected from bright lights, and I was given a pair of sunglasses. I expected that when I put them on, I would see all the frames around the eyes with both eyes so that it would be like looking through two tubes. I, of course, didn't see that and was amazed that the vision of my two eyes was unified in the center.

Near Christmas of that year my brother and I began exploring a closet in the bedroom and found some toys stored there. My mother quickly told us not to be exploring any further and we didn't. That Christmas I got a tricycle that I thought was great.

I started school in 1949 and was taken to school that first day by my mother. I liked it and did well, but I was in the second row as a class sub-group and thought that the first group must have been a smarter group of students. That, most probably, wasn't true, but that was my impression and may have affected my perceptions of my capabilities. I remember the teacher talking about Truman being elected as president. I don't remember much else about that first-year classroom, but I did like recess and playing around a thicket of blackberry vines at the far end of the play yard. A teacher would ring a handheld bell to signal the start of class. The cafeteria was on the lower level of the school near the restrooms and often served stewed prunes. I remember liking them, with their sweet taste, very well.

On Halloween during our stay in the farm home, we (the family) were outside in a portion of the cow lot near a pile of firewood. The large and beautiful full Moon rose in the sky fully visible from where we were gathered. As I watched, I seemed to see the vision of a black clothed and hatted witch riding a broom across the face of the moon. It was very real to men at the time, but I certainly have not seen anything like that since.

Through my daddy's employment we were provided healthcare through the local clinic and hospital mentioned earlier. My brother and I were taken there for our immunizations. Whenever they were administered, we were taken to a room that had rough cloth pads covering places where we would have to lie down face-down with our buttocks exposed. The shots were then administered using what seemed to be large needles. These weren't the one-time-use needles of today. They were larger and thicker, and they hurt. Several "shots" were administered to us in this manner, and I dreaded all of them. We also got a smallpox vaccination on our upper arm. I didn't mind that, because it was administered with the edges of a broken glass vial that barely pricked the skin. Later, a strange scab appeared there, and a smallpox scar remained after healing, that became almost like a "badge of honor" later when all the others had one.

We later got a polio vaccination with the newly available Salk Vaccine; this was a wonderful and, in many cases, "lifesaving" development. There weren't many cases of Polio around De Queen, but in the city of Texarkana there were significant numbers of cases, and "Iron lungs" were in use then. Later there was the Sabine vaccine which was taken orally.

CHAPTER TWO
CHAPEL HILL

In the summer after my first school year, the family bought a small ten-acre farm about three miles west of De Queen and about one-quarter mile south of U.S. Highway 70. The farm was located at the corner of the dirt road leading from the highway. The road, at that point, was a clay hill for the last 200 yards. At the bottom of the hill, a small creek crossed the road and there was no way across the creek except to drive through it, or when walking, to wade across it or try to jump from one spot of land to another. When wet, the clay hill became almost impassable. Daddy brought metal "slag" pieces from where he worked and put them into ruts created in the hill, hoping to improve traction for the pickup tires as he climbed the hill daily. He later bought some "mud grip" tires for the pickup and I guess that helped, but not enough. Eventually, he went and talked with the county commissioner and the county paved the road with gravel and installed a culvert at the creek crossing.

That first year on the farm my brother and I rode a school bus that ran on the highway. We had to walk the quarter-mile road, cross the creek, and wait for the bus at the highway. There was no shelter for us near the highway and that meant standing in the rain, when it was raining, to catch the bus. To provide us some shelter, daddy procured some "slab" lumber from a local sawmill and built a shelter. Slabs are pieces of tree wood that are the first pieces cut from logs as they are sawed in a sawmill. They have the bark on one side and are uneven in thickness and width but have one flat even side which can be used for an attachment surface. That shelter must have looked atrocious to the neighbor who lived at that junction of the access road and the highway as it wasn't long before a grass fire from that neighbor's place burned through the area and burned down the makeshift shelter. It was not rebuilt.

Hwy. 70 was, again, a blacktop highway running from central Arkansas, then westward into Oklahoma. The state line was about six miles away: notable because beer could be purchased there (Sevier County Arkansas was "Dry"), but, also, notable to me, because Rock Creek was crossed by the highway at the state line. It was a landmark to me as we often traveled into Oklahoma, passing through Eagletown (Why the name? I don't know.), then on westward across the Mountain Fork River to Broken Bow, outside of which was my daddy's parents' home.

The Rolling Fork River lay about two miles west of the farm. That river, and all its water flows and fishing holes, became an important (and often used) element of life in Chapel Hill. Hwy 70 crossed the river on a concrete bridge and the right-of-way on the sides of the bridge provided access, but the banks were steep and sometimes slippery. Boats could be tied below the bridge if one really wanted to leave one unattended. Years later, a couple of college friends and I, on a lark, went to the river at the bridge and found a homemade boat, which had been fashioned from two old 1940's style car hoods welded together, partially submerged under the bridge. We emptied the water out of it and paddled it out on the water for a while as it leaked water, then left it where we found it.

The home and its ten acres lay on the crest of a hill with the house being sited near the apex. A giant Red Oak tree that must have been at least 150 years old grew in front of the house and provided a lot of shade for the house in the afternoons. A Holly tree, with its red berries in winter, grew a few yards from the oak. A Sweet Gum tree, with its large delta-spiked and very green leaves, and its green, then brown and spiked, seed balls, grew a few yards from the Holly tree. Other Red Oak trees grew down the hill side providing shade for the entire area, which became the circular driveway for the home autos. Two White Oak trees grew to the east of the hillside oaks and were notable for their white-tinged bark and the size of their acorns. Two large Pecan trees, that had to have been planted by the farm's previous owner, grew in a fenced garden area to the south of the house. Some lower limbs had been partially trimmed to keep them from contacting the ground and restricting access under the trees. Both trees continued to bear nuts during all my years there. A small orchard with six to eight fruit trees grew beyond the Pecan trees. These lasted a few years, but never bore any usable fruit.

A shed (this was a smokehouse intended for curing meat), sat in the yard about ten yards away from the back porch of the house. Inside long poles spanned the space between the walls, these were obviously intended for hanging meat that was being cured by heat and smoke but were never used by the family for that purpose. In the center of the shed's floor was a spot with charred edges that had obviously caught fire at some time past. No attempt to repair the hole was ever made.

The entry step in front of the entry door was a single block of limestone about ten inches high and about a foot wide; that step was used, subsequently, for many purposes, including cracking hickory nuts with a hammer. Later, when my brother and I became teenagers, a basketball goal was affixed above the door and used very often. The wall behind the goal was, really, not suitable for a basketball goal backboard, but that made no difference for us when shooting for goals or playing against each other.

The other outbuilding in the yard area was a partially enclosed "washhouse" where the new electric washing machine was installed and used. The source of water for the family was the water well which was there and encircled by the concrete flooring. A large dark red ceramic tile (about 3 feet inside diameter) formed the top of the well and other tiles lined its depth into the bottom. The top tile protruded only about 10 inches above the surrounding concrete surface. This was deemed insufficient by my daddy, who constructed a square wood rail fence around the top. The first rail was about a foot above the surface of the top tile. For whatever reason, one morning as I was drawing water to take back into the kitchen, I felt drawn to the well and I peered down into the dark shaft to see the surface of the water mirroring the reflection of light off the surface of the water. As I peered down, I felt the urge to jump into the well, and even extended my leg over the first rail, preparing to swing my body over that rail and drop into the water (about 30 feet). At the precipice, I pulled back and then went about completing my task. That urge never returned – until years later, as a young adult visiting relative in Dallas. We went to the observation deck of a tall office building downtown where, as I peered down from the retaining wall at the building's edge, I felt the urge to leap out into the space above the street below. I forced myself to pull away from the wall and have never had a similar urge since, but I don't like being near drop-offs of any sort.

Second Grade

I started my Second-Grade school year in a different school due to the location of our new home; this was Central Elementary School and was newer than the Rose Hill Elementary school I had attended the previous year. My teacher was Mrs. Pullen, she was a grayish woman whose belly protruded slightly, and the belt of her dresses was often below her waistline in the front. She also had a hawkish look about her. She gave the class instructions that we were to always have two pencils on our desk. At the supper table I brought that instruction to the attention of the family. My daddy immediately said "Baloney" and I didn't get the extra pencil. Soon thereafter, Mrs. Pullen came by my desk and saw that I didn't have the extra pencil. She asked why I didn't have it. I told her "My daddy said Baloney." She, soon thereafter, came by my desk with the stub of a pencil, this one having a square eraser holder on the top. My mother has since stated that when she visited my room with the PTA that Mrs. Pullen gave her the oddest look, which she didn't understand.

As an aside, about fifty years later, when visiting my parents, the subject came up in conversation and I told them what Mrs. Pullen had done about the extra pencil. After my daddy said

"Well, there was no note from the teacher." I told him he didn't get off that easily. I didn't tell him this, but in my opinion he did it because he had a chance to be mean, and, particularly, to be mean to me, who he had shown evidence of having a strong dislike for. My daddy, in subsequent conversation said, "Do you want me to get you a pencil?" I thought, when he said that, it was very perceptive on his part to realize that the resolution to this affair was for him to give me a pencil, despite it being years and years later. I said, "Yes, and I'll take it and put it on her grave "– something I had been thinking about for a long time. He turned away and nothing further was said.

There was a time, during our first year in the Chapel Hill home, when, in the early evening, I was on the north side of the house doing whatever and I think my brother was close by; my daddy, who had his shift changed at the creosote plant, came by and said, "The Lord changed my shift so I can take care of you." I took that to mean that, somehow, I was doing something wrong, or that I was somehow not acting right; I later was told by my mother that my daddy's mother, who had been/was a Holiness preacher, had said she didn't like me; that I was not like the others and was "Too proud." That was bound to have had an influence on my daddy in his actions toward me.

A Cold Winter

During that winter, in early February, the weather turned very cold and almost a foot of snow fell on the area. My school, Central Elementary where I was in the second grade, was located about four blocks north of the town square. The natural gas supply to heat the central boiler for the in-room radiator system was turned off, or there was insufficient supply to keep it in operation. Our school classes were shifted to the basement of the First Baptist Church, which was on the same north-south street, but one block south of the city square. We walked (marched?), class-by-class, along the snow-covered sidewalks to the church where we found tables set up in a well-lit large room for us to do our work. I easily adapted to this new situation and proceeded to work on my lessons. I specifically remember eating my lunch, a biscuit with some content inside wrapped in foil. I had other items included in my lunch, of course, but my memory fails me on that detail. This arrangement lasted three to four days.

When winter weather systems came through the home area, the pattern for precipitation was usually rain, then freezing rain, then snow, if we got any. The result was that the branches of all the trees around the home and the forest became coated with ice. Later, when the sun returned, the sunlight glinted off the limbs of the trees and made the area appear as a crystal forest. As the ice melted, it fell in shards from the trees that appeared as mini showers of crystals.

The new house was certainly nicer than the previous one, but it still had a fireplace in the living room as the heating source for most of the house and only a cook stove in the kitchen. This didn't work well, and a better cooking stove was needed in the kitchen to replace the kerosene stove that was still in use. The kitchen had a brick chimney for a wood cookstove, with a connection point for the smoke pipe from the stove located high up on one wall, but installing a wood cookstove was never, apparently, a considered option. Instead, a decision was made to install a butane gas heating system in the house and in the kitchen.

My daddy proceeded to dig a large rectangular hole in the side yard outside the kitchen for a large tank necessary for underground storage of the Butane fuel. The hole was, again, very well dug, with sharply defined corners and smooth vertical walls about six feet deep (like the grave dug previously). The tank was delivered and soon buried, connecting pipes were run underground to the kitchen, dining room, and living room. A new (not new, used but in good condition) gas cooking range was installed in the kitchen, a small floor heater with radiant brickettes was installed in the dining room, and a larger, console style heater was installed in the living room. This system seemed to work well, and Mom certainly appreciated the new cookstove.

Later, the cost of the butane was deemed to be quite expensive, and a wood-burning floor stove was installed in the living room. It had a pipe that was ducted through the wall above the fireplace into the existing fireplace chimney. The first stove installed there was an inexpensive one that had thin metal construction. As the fire inside burned, the outside of the thin metal sheeting would begin to glow red where the hot coals on the inside were contacting the outside metal. That stove was replaced the next year with a cast iron stove that was much more serviceable. Eventually, it became my task in the mornings to build a fire in the stove soon after I had risen from bed and dressed. I became very proficient at quickly building those fires.

The wood stove, as a main heating source, necessitated a lot of effort to procure a wood supply, process it into useable size wood and move it to the front porch where it could be easily accessed when needed for the fire. Much of the homesite transport from the wood pile (of various types) was done by stacking the "sticks" onto a small "toy" red wagon, then pulling and pushing it up the hill to the front porch of the house. That "toy" wagon, which was about three feet long, maybe fourteen inches high, with eight-inch wheels and a long tongue with a handle in the end. It was used for lots of purposes around the home that had nothing to do with child's play.

One of those tasks was transporting cow feed from the pickup to the storage area in the cow lot. Those burlap sacks weighed at least fifty pounds and were difficult to maneuver out of the truck bed and onto the wagon for the two of us, then we had to unload it and move it into the storage area. We did develop some skill in opening the sacks by raveling the twine that sealed the sacks. This could be done by loosening the twine at one end of the sack, then pulling it away from the seam for the entire length of the sack in one motion. The other side of the twine could then be pulled free, thus easily opening the sacks. To make this system work, the correct end had to be the one chosen, sometimes that was a matter of trial-and-error before the sacks could be successfully opened. That twine had many uses, including providing amusement by us trying to form a "Jacob's Ladder" lattice with the twine strung between our hands. We never mastered that skill, but we tried often, partly out of boredom, I guess. The burlap feed bags "Tow Sacks," we called them, also had many uses on the farm.

To provide a wood supply, one year daddy secured a lot of the "slabs," mentioned earlier. To cut those slabs into useable lengths, he rigged up a bench saw that was to be powered by the pickup using a large flat, sawmill style, belt to transfer the power from the truck to the saw. After constructing the saw, using a circular blade, an axle shaft and its bearings, and the wood frame on which all of this was mounted, he was ready to cut the wood. I believe the frame also included a moveable carriage that allowed the slab to be placed on it and fed into the saw as the cut was made.

To adapt the pickup truck, that was to be used as a power source, Daddy had a section of round steel pipe welded to a truck tire rim (the same one that cut my leg?) without a tire on it. The rear axle of the truck was jacked up on the left side, the truck's rear wheel tire assembly removed. The rim, with the steel pipe pulley on it, was bolted onto the truck axle. When the truck engine was then started, and the drivetrain activated, the revolution speed of the engine (RPM) was set by using a manual throttle, which was a feature of the truck at that time - a 1949 Chevrolet. The differential in the axle allowed the one off-the-ground wheel to spin, while the other was stationary on the ground thusly driving the belt and turning the saw blade. The system worked well, and the slabs were cut as desired, however this system was not used again after this one time.

The Water System

As mentioned previously, the well was the water source for the family. At first the "bucket and rope" system was used to draw water, but the time soon came to improve that system. A trip to Texarkana, to Burman Pharr hardware found a pump system that would work. All the upper parts were painted red, and it had a long, about four-foot, operating handle. A lower cylinder, with a one-way valve on the bottom, was attached to steel pipe and placed deep into the well water. The cylinder piston was operated by a rod extending through the pipe from the pump upper part structure and was attached to the long handle of the large red pump. There was a spigot about midway up the upper pump's structure and a bucket could be hung on the spigot. As the pump handle was operated, the water would flow out of the spigot into the bucket. Many pump strokes were required to fill the bucket.

Later, it was decided to adapt the pump system to provide running water inside the home. A frame was made of cedar posts about twelve feet in length – these were cut from the local forest and placed upright outside the washhouse, close to the pump. A large circular steel tank was procured and placed on top of the cedar post tower. Then a connection to the pump was made using an opening in the pump wall opposite the spigot. A steel pipe was threaded into the pump connection and extended to the top of the outside tank. This provided a system to pump water into the tank using the large red pump. A funnel was formed to connect the end of the fill pipe into the tank by using a steel vegetable can and fitting it into an opening in the top of the tank. Adding water to the tank became a daily chore for my brother and I, and a certain number of pump handle "strokes," usually fifty, was often used as punishment for whatever transgression we were deemed to have committed. I pumped a lot of strokes, but sometimes my brother and I, due to boredom, or whatever, pumped the tank full to the overrunning point, partly to avoid having to do the daily filling chore for a few days.

The pump handle left me with a permanent reminder of its existence, by once chipping my left front tooth, when I rapidly raised the end of the handle, and it struck me in my face. I was careful not to do that again. The platform we stood on while pumping water consisted of two large limestone slabs about six inches thick. The fossilized remains of prehistoric marine animals were clearly visible on the surface of the stones.

A steel pipe of three-quarter inch inside diameter, was attached to the bottom of the tank and ran down into the ground extended to the house, then brought up, through the floor, into the kitchen. An outdoor style faucet was attached to the pipe near the preexisting sink and, "presto" the home had running water. Another pipe was also run from the bottom of the tank over into the back area of the washhouse. A showerhead nozzle was attached, giving the family an outside way of taking a shower, instead of bathing in a washtub inside the house. That shower was a welcome addition to the home conveniences and the water was pleasant to shower under because the water in the tower had been heated by the Sun during the daytime.

The Clothes Washing Operation

This was a labor intense operation and was performed tirelessly by my mother, who had all the other household tasks to do as well.

The clothes washer: the new electric one with the "wringer" (that wasn't new, but certainly was a prominent feature of the machine and the operation), was located in the washhouse, along with a sturdy bench and two galvanized, No. 2 sized, washtubs. The washing machine had to be filled with hot water and then the detergent (notably: "Tide") was added to that. The wash tubs (used for rinsing only) had to each be filled with clear unheated water, about ten gallons each. All that water had to be drawn, or rather "pumped," out of the well a couple of gallons, or less, at a time.

The water for the washing machine had to be heated. The way that was done, was to use a large cast iron "washpot" located in the yard outside of the washhouse. The pot had to be filled with water, then a wood fire was built around the pot. When hot, the water had to be dipped out of the pot and carried into the washhouse and poured, bucketful by bucketful, into the washing machine. The clothes washing operation could then begin. Washing began with the whites: sheets, towels, etc., as the first load. Sometimes "bluing" was added to the water in the first rinse to prevent yellowing of the white items. The items were passed individually through the wringer and into the next rinse, until finally being wrung into a basket for transporting to the clotheslines to be hung for drying in the open air. The process was repeated until all the items had been washed, rinsed, then hung to dry. Upon completion, all the water in the washer and the tubs had to then be removed; this was done by using a drain hose from the washer emptying into a drain in the floor of the wash house that carried the water out into the yard where it emptied onto the open ground. Then the tubs were emptied by dipping out the water until they could be carried and emptied by hand.

The Baby Raccoon

During the summer of that first year in Chapel hill, the family, on one afternoon, went over to Rolling Fork River and drove in the pickup along the old gravel highway that went from Chapel Hill on over into Oklahoma. The road leading the last half mile to the bridge had, in essence, been abandoned by the county highway department but the road was still passable and continued to an old iron bridge across the river. When we were there, a mama raccoon and her babies came onto the bridge from the opposite end. My daddy proceeded to catch one of the babies, which was about the size of a cat, and we brought it home.

We didn't have a cage and the only place to keep the small racoon was at the bottom of an extra ceramic tile that was sitting in the yard out behind the washhouse. The inside vertical slick sides of the tile, which the baby couldn't grab with its claws, served to make the enclosure inescapable. For whatever reason, I felt compelled to help the young animal and I placed a bucket, with its bottom up, on the ground inside the tile. When I returned the young animal was gone, which was probably the best outcome for the young raccoon. Nothing was ever said about the escape, as I recall.

The Lawn Mower

This was about the time when we got our first lawn mower. Before this, the only way to cut the grass was to use a wood-handled sling blade device that would cut grass on both of the back-and-forth strokes. It had a wide foot-long blade that had rippled edges that could be sharpened with a standard file. The resulting grass surface was, generally, very uneven but reduced in height. The lawn mower was purchased at an auction of household goods, and I think the selling price was fifty cents.

The mower was a well-used hand-pushed reel mower, but its purchase represented a "step up" for the family. My brother and I split the duties of mowing the yard by each taking, what was roughly, half of the yard. We mowed the yard weekly to keep it looking good. There was a section in the back that was terraced, and it was best mowed by, repeatedly mowing down the slope, pulling the mower backwards up the slope, then cutting another swath by pushing it down the slope again.

My brother and I did all this mowing quite willingly and took pride in keeping the yard nicely mowed. It was years before a gasoline engine powered rotary mower was used. There were gasoline powered reel mowers at the time, but those were only used in the town as far as I know.

CHAPTER THREE
PINEY GROVE BIBLE CAMP

There was an old (and unpainted) church, with its steeple and hand-rung bell in the Chapel Hill community. It sat on a high point (really the upper plateau) in the community– hence the name "Chapel Hill." During Christmas of our first year there, a community gathering in celebration of Christmas was held in the church. There was, I believe, someone dressed up as Santa Claus, and I remember cellophane bags of nuts and hard ribbon candies, and maybe an orange in the bags also. I certainly got mine and I remember the sweet taste of the candies.

This church was also the voting place for the community, and I remember my daddy commenting that Mama had gotten a poll tax and was going to vote, or did vote, in that election. Poll taxes have since been ruled unconstitutional because it was a means of voter suppression. We didn't attend church services there, but, instead, it was chosen that we attend services at a nearby place Called Piney Grove Bible Camp, which was located on the north side of Hwy 70, back toward the town of De Queen. The camp, sited on about 20 acres of land bordering the highway, had a grove of about 20 very large Loblolly Pine trees around the center site, and numerous other smaller pine trees in, what once had been, an open field east of the larger grove – hence the name "Piney Grove," I guess.

I never fully understood who owned the camp, but it seemed to be to be to be run by an evangelical group out of Dallas, Texas associated with a minister and radio personality, W.E. Hawkins. That group organized and held two summer camps for children and youths who came mainly from the Dallas area, and some from Paris, Texas.

A Night in the Woods

There was a caretaker who resided on the property whose name was, I believe, Mr. Pierce. One fall Saturday evening, shortly after the family started attending church services there, he took several community boys, including me, on an outing into the woods and drove us, in his old Model A Ford, out about five miles west on the highway, then turned north onto a gravel road running into the forest. The road had once been, in earlier years, a part of the gravel highway system leading off into Oklahoma. After a short distance on the gravel road, he drove the car off into the woods for probably one quarter of a mile. There, a bonfire was lit, and we probably roasted wieners on sharpened forked sticks cut from small tree limbs.

After the wiener roast, we played a game, which is a variation of "Hide and Seek" called "Kick the Can." In the game, someone was chosen as "It" (the seeker) and the rest would run and hide, this time in the darkness of the forest. When a player was "found," he had to go stand in a circle back at the starting point. A tin can was set up in the middle of the circle, and if any player could sneak back up to the circle, without being detected by the seeker, and "kick the can," then all the players who had been found could run free, thusly starting the game all over again. The game required vigilance over the area near the circle by the seeker while also seeking hiders and any players who might be sneaking back to free the found players. It also required stealth on the part of the hiders who would have to move and maintain concealment as they sneaked back towards the circle. Perhaps, by requiring stealth, cunning, vigilance and brazenness, not to mention overcoming fears of being in the dark in a strange forest, this was a lesson in real-life events to come.

The Summer Camps

Other than the caretaker's cottage, there was an old two-story house near the grove of large pines that served as the girl's dormitory during the camps and the meeting place for the small congregation for church services. The house had an upstairs and a covered balcony which served as a sleeping place for many of the girls during the camps. Another outbuilding, lying sort of between the two-story house and the caretaker's cottage, was a large open-air building without sides that had a sawdust floor, large pine poles around the perimeter for support of the roof and wooden slotted benches (with back rests) for pews. It was called "The Tabernacle." The camps used this building for assemblages of the campers, and the local families used it for weekly Sunday services during the summer months. Another (enclosed) meeting building was under construction near the eastern edge of the piney grove, out in front of the two-story house. This new building would later serve as a larger congregational meeting space during the colder months.

There were two "camps" each summer: the June Camp and the August Camp, each occurring about mid-month. The girls and women were housed in the old two-story house, which had a large balcony across the front that was a sleeping area, and the men and boys were housed in semi-open bunk house, located across a small open field east of the main complex. It stood amid a lightly forested area of small pine and older oak trees. My brother and I got to attend the camps, but never slept in the bunkhouse. Instead, I took a cot, placed it in an open area under the trees, with my extra clothing in an old valise style bag my daddy had brought home from the Navy that I placed under the cot. I slept in the open forest for those nights. I didn't have a fear of anything coming at me during the night and, as best as I can remember, slept quite well. Luckily, during the June camps, there was never any rain, from which I was totally unprotected.

I always enjoyed the breakfasts, served on long tables to the campers. Scrambled eggs were my favorite food, and I was hungry after the long nights. The shower bathing was done in a small shed behind the enclosed new building that had a slotted raised wood floor, but no drains. Once, in a later year's camp, it was reported that a teen-age girl had discovered a window in the adjacent building that provided a view of the shower entrance, and often unclothed males could easily be seen from that window. Reportedly, an older teenager gave her a full view.

At one of my first camps, with all the activities, I found no necessity to shower. My daddy saw me on the third day and told me to shower and change clothes. I remember also attending that camp "barefooted," as we normally were during the summer; I had, prior to the camp, gotten a barb (sticker) planted in the bottom of my foot and I walked only on the heel to avoid the pair in the barb. I was told to rub some alcohol on the sticker site, and I did so. Shortly thereafter the pair subsided, and I could walk normally, but still barefooted.

To provide cool water for the campers, in one of the later years camps, a block ice cooling system was devised and installed. A shallow pit was dug near an outside water outlet and a copper pipe coil was placed in the bottom of the shallow hole. A large, probably 50 pounds, block of ice was placed on the coil and the hole was covered. As the water circulated through the copper coil it was cooled by the melting ice and provided campers with cool water to drink.

These camps were attended by children and teens from the Dallas-Fort Worth area, and other areas in Texas and, consequently, gave us some exposure to people outside of the small area in which we lived. Some of those exposures resulted in longer term relationships among the teenage campers. My next younger brother met a girl, formed a relationship and later they married. There were other personalities who attended the camps. I remember "Uncle Steve" and "Brother Price" and his family. The camp and the local attendees' services were supported by the Dallas Theological Seminary and students drove in weekly to support the services for the local attendees. A notable couple was "Bob and Pearl' who took a long-term interest in the families who were at the camp and the local church that was later formed for those families.

During the year when I was in the Third Grade, a self-styled missionary sort of person: a young man with a last name of

"Kirby" was there and, after whatever service, gathered the young people into a back room (I think it was an original kitchen, and took us through a semi-ritual of "Leading us to the Lord," i.e., becoming "Christians." My older brother and I were in the group, along with other boys in the area (I don't remember any girls), and, unwittingly I guess, participated in the ritual and were "Saved." Afterward, my brother and I went home and, once there, I felt very happy and, apparently, so did my brother. My mother later told me our faces were "shining." I have no explanation for any of this, but the younger brother of one of the boys, who was in my class, at school, said, out on the playground during recess the next day, that his older brother had been "Saved." I thought it best not to comment, or reveal, my own experiences.

CHAPTER FOUR
ROLLING FORK RIVER

The river starts, as previously mentioned, in Polk County, Arkansas and flows south through the mountainous terrain of the Ouachita Mountains near the Oklahoma border into the semi-hilly area and flatter (river bottom) areas of Sevier County, Arkansas. Some recent maps I have seen give the name presented as Rolling Fork Creek. I find that to be a slighting of the size and length of this water channel that I have spent so much time with when growing up. Rolling Fork eventually flows into Little River in the southern part of Sevier County and is paralleled in its' southward flow, by the Cossatot and the Saline Rivers in Arkansas, and In Oklahoma, by the Mountain Fork and Glover Rivers. All these rivers are part of the Mississippi watershed. The portions of the river most accessed by my family and I were in the transition zone between the rocky foothills of the Ouachita Mountains and the flatter, bottom lands of the lower part. The water was for the most part semi clear, free from contamination, and teaming with various species of fish. There were bream, sun perch, large-mouth bass, rock bass, yellow catfish, channel catfish, and the occasional drum. Crappies were present, I'm sure, but we never caught one that I know of. Later, when De Queen Lake was formed my mother and daddy caught Crappie in the deep still waters of the inlets.

To fish on the river, we needed a boat (although we did a lot of fishing from the banks), and not having the funds to buy a metal Jon boat, my daddy set about to build a boat for us to use. He started out by building a protype made of rough, thin wood planking for the bottom and sides. It was probably about 10 feet long and seemed a sturdy-enough craft for its size. We tried it on one of the two small ponds on the farm. The one nearest the home was in the calf pasture, as we called it, and was a shallow pond dug by the previous owners probably using horses and a small dredge to scoop out the earth and form the dam. In the spring it was filled with runoff water from the pasture and, when we slipped the boat into the water, it was completely full. The boat worked quite well and was stable enough for our use. I often paddled the boat around the pond and that gave me a lot of experience in handling a small watercraft.

In the late spring, or early summer, when the river was still flowing relatively swiftly from the spring rains, my daddy, my brother, and I took that boat over to Rolling Fork to a place called "McRae's Crossing." We loaded the boat into the bed of the pickup, with the tailgate down and a tire placed under the boat to cushion it and hold it steady, then we drove to the river. The first sight of the river was from a bluff at a bend in the river that was about 40 feet above the water and supported a grove of those very tall pine trees that were common in that part of the country. The road(?) then turned right and worked its way through deeply sided dirt passages to the river crossing, which was a gravel-bottomed shoal area that afforded a hard-bottom river crossing to the farmland on the other side of the river.

Years afterwards, I played golf with my old junior High school football coach, when I mentioned Mc Rae's crossing in our conversation, and he immediately began talking about that crossing and told me his father had farmed some land on the other side of the river. He also told me that they used to go fishing and used tow sacks with crushed walnut husks in them to catch the fish. The husk filled sacks were thrown into the water and weighted (I'm sure) to get them to sink down to the bottom, the acid in the husks was released and the fish would boil up to the surface to escape the acid. The fish were then scooped out of the water. Seems a bit "fishy' to me, but whatever.

When we arrived at the river, it was still in the semi-flood stage and the water at the crossing was about two feet deep and not suitable for crossing. It was, however, suitable for fishing with the trotline that my daddy had planned to set out. A trotline is constructed by using a long sturdy cord that is strung between two stationary points on the banks and securely tied to those points. Shorter cords, about two–three feet long, with hooks on the ends are then tied a few feet on the longer stringing cord. The hooks are baited and then left to be found by the fish.

The line was strung from the base of a tree, and probably tied to an exposed tree root, across the inlet of a small stream which emptied into the river. The other end was secured by tying it to a small tree. The line was left in place and a return to the river to run the line and check for fish was planned for that night after my daddy completed his work shift at the creosote plant.

That night my brother and I did not go to bed, rather lay waiting for daddy's return on the sides of a divan in the living room that had been laid flat in a double bed configuration. This divan was covered with an early version of plastic, which, I'm sure that made it more affordable for my parents, but it didn't last for very long. For whatever reason in the mind of a seven-year-old young boy, I thought it important to sleep in the same position as my brother. I fell asleep and when we were awakened later, my position was of course, completely different.

We loaded into the pickup and set out in the middle of the night for the river. I remember the moon on that night was a fat crescent in the eastern sky and had the yellow cast of a Last Quarter Moon. We had a flashlight with us that had been made of a glow-in-the-dark plastic that would stay glowing softly for about ten to fifteen minutes after being exposed to a strong light source. We also had a kerosene lantern, which gave off a yellow light from the flame burning off the exposed wick under its glass protector.

We boarded our small boat and proceeded to run the trotline in the swiftly flowing brownish green water. We pulled up the trotline and worked our way along its length, which could not have been more than 15 yards end to end. We found a few fish, mostly small catfish, on our hooks. I'm sure we took those home and Daddy cleaned them that night. Mom probably fried them for breakfast the next morning, but that's not part of my memory. This was the only time that we set a trotline, and we didn't do any more fishing at night. We did some night fishing at another time earlier, but that's another story.

We later did a lot of fishing on this river, and we used a longer and heavier boat that my daddy later built using more substantial materials of thicker planed lumber; it was sealed with tar and painted green. That boat was heavy, and it took my brother and I together on the smaller front end to carry it from the truck to the water, and, of course, load it back in the truck for the trip home. We often returned to McRae's Crossing and fished both upriver and downriver from the crossing; downriver was better for fishing. The strong current, even when the river was at a normal level, made the trip down to a bend in the river, where the water was still in places and lily pads grew, an easy one, but, of course, returning upriver against the current required some strong paddling. We often fished in the still waters of the bend and caught a lot of bream which are small perch-like fish and tasty when fried, but, occasionally, picked up some catfish, and small bass.

At other times, we waded in the river and fished. We used only cane poles when fishing and had no other means to do our fishing. I was wading (as a teenager) near the bank in the bend area across from the high bluff and fishing with my cane pole about ten feet away, and I caught a few fish, including a sucker fish called a "Red Horse" due to its bright red color. I released it back into the water.

The family used the area upstream of the crossing for a "swimming hole" and it was suitable due to its rocky bottom for an extended distance upriver. My brother and I somehow got a diving mask and used it to investigate an outcropping in the bottom under about five feet of water, that closely resembled the roots and trunk of a petrified tree. It seemed to be made of rock and had the shape of the base of a tree with a hollow portion in the center of the trunk, but we never found out what it really was. At one time, when I was about 13, I decided I wanted to swim some after we had been fishing. I had no swim shorts, so I swam naked, but I was very uneasy about being naked in front of my brother and my daddy. I never repeated that again.

We dug redworms out of a region in the back yard and put them in a can to take with us when we went fishing, but Daddy got a seine net, mounted on some short poles on both ends and we seined for some live bait before we fished, especially at the crossing. It worked well and we used this live bait, some shad minnows, some other fish, to catch bigger fish.

Other areas of the river were fished as well: there was a long straight channel that lay mostly south of the Highway 70 bridge. It was called "Cane Hole." The water around and below the bridge was deep, how deep I never knew, but some large rocks were visible underwater close to the bridge at the point where we launched the boat. My daddy often caught a "Rock Bass" or two near those rocks. My older brother once caught a good-sized largemouth bass on his rod and reel with a "scissortail" yellow lure. My brother had been given the rod and reel some time previously by my parents. We fished along the banks, particularly the west bank a lot, but I never remember catching very many fish there.

Launching that heavy boat onto the river at the bridge was always a difficult task. The boat was heavy, the slope was steep and often slippery due to the wetness of the clay bank. A large handle had been mounted on the bow, which my brother and I both grasped, and my daddy had two handles on the rear, larger, end which he handled by himself. Of course, taking the boat out of the river and placing it back into the bed of the pickup truck was an even harder task. Despite the heaviness and all the difficulty, my brother and I willingly did our best and always accomplished our tasks.

In later years, we would go to another fishing hole, north of the bridge and about a mile and a half upriver. It was called "Blue Hole," why that name? I have no idea, it didn't seem blue to me. It, again, had a steep bank on the entry (west) side that had to be negotiated to launch the boat, but the fishing was good, and we visited often to fish and swim. Later, another youth, my older brother and I returned here intending to spend the night on the river, but, after I cooked our supper (fried steak) in a skillet over an open fire, we decided to go back home. That was probably a good decision; after experiencing two nights previously camping out near the crossing and being miserable sleeping in the cab of the truck, and we were poorly equipped to camp this last time.

During that previous camping trip at McRae's Crossing, I remember the owls in the nearby trees hooting during the night, and cooking potatoes and wieners for our lunch by boiling them over an open fire. We fished some during that trip, but it was off the bank only. The youth that was with us hooked an eel near the bend of the river. I had never seen an eel in the river before, or since. This one wrapped itself around the root of a tree that grew horizontally close to the water and thus prevented its capture. I don't know what we would have done with the eel if we had captured it, or how we would have removed the hook and released it. As it was, the line broke and prevented its capture. There was nothing more we could do.

Johnson's Bridge

There was another place on the river that was virtually the county swimming hole. It was located further north from Blue Hole and was a large area of rocky shores and river bottom on the east side of the river with a high bluff, about 15 feet high on the other side. All these features, plus the clean clear water that flowed from the northern mountainous area into this spot made the area perfect for swimming. The high bluff was accessible only by swimming across the river. Once on the bluff (there was a place to climb from the river) one had a choice of jumping upright into the water, or diving. Not many chose to dive. When jumping, the impact of the water was still quite severe, but some had discovered that jumping into an area where someone else had just jumped lessened that impact, because the air bubbles created by the first jumper made the water less dense. I remember an older teenage girl talking about that to the young men she was with. She called it "Breaking Water."

The bridge required a wide span to extend from the high ground on the east side, to the bluff on the west side. It was a modern (for that time) concrete bridge and, at the place where it spanned the water, it was about 35 feet above it. At that high point, two concrete pillars with flat tops stood close together. This point was the chosen place where the youths would stand before plunging into the river below. One afternoon I decided that I was going to "take the plunge" and jump off the bridge. I went out onto the bridge and hesitantly climbed onto the two posts and stood there considering the consequences for a short while, but then stepped off into the void. The fall seemed to take a long time before I hit the water. I don't recall the impact with the water being greater than that when jumping off the bluff, but I never did that again.

When the family first visited the bridge, shortly after the time we moved to Chapel Hill, it was under construction. On that afternoon Daddy drove the pickup truck out onto an expanse of rocky shoreline north of the bridge that was close to where the water at line started. We played in the shallow water that slowly deepened as we waded into it. All was well, until we started to leave the area. The rocky surface hid the fact that the water level of the river was just under the surface. The tires of the pickup broke through that upper layer into the wet layer below and the truck became stuck. Daddy went over to the bridge construction site and returned with one or two broad boards and successfully used those to free the truck. As the sun was setting, we left the area.

CHAPTER FIVE
HOME LIFE ON THE FARM

The small farm we lived on was just ten acres, but, in addition to the river, my brother and I had all the surrounding countryside for our use, exploration and enjoyment. Those properties varied from open fields to thick woods and there was no thought of trespassing or restricted areas, other than around homesites themselves, and that was for respecting privacy reasons (although we never thought of it in those terms). The field in front of our house even became our baseball field, where we would play a game called "Flies and Skinners" and later, when there were enough of us, actual games of softball.

"Flies and Skinners" was played by having one person being the batter, then the others would be fielders. The batter would toss the ball in the air, then, as it dropped, hit it with the bat. Some hit balls flew (flies), and some were ground balls (skinners). When enough flies, usually three, and/or enough skinners were fielded by a player (usually six), he then became the batter. It was a very good way of developing baseball skills. Even today, when I am on the golf course and a ball happens to be headed toward me, I'm thinking of moving toward the ball to catch it, rather than away toward safety. We also had to search for balls that fell in the tall grass to keep our game going and preserve the balls for future use.

In the summers, we would make weekly tours of the surrounding fields and woods gathering blackberries as they ripened. Afterwards we would have to take baths in water mixed with pine detergent (Pine Sol) to kill the chiggers we would have picked up on legs and clothing. The blackberries were part of our food supply, and some would be canned for later use.

Night Fishing

On a summer night in the first, or second year that we lived in Chapel Hill, my daddy took my older brother and me on a night-fishing adventure along a creek north of Highway 70, not far from, and to the east of the point where our access road joined the highway. The land belonged to, I believe, the Weaver family who had an open field around their house, then wooded areas all around. The creek was in the woods, in a valley to the east of the home. We took our kerosene (we called it coal oil) lantern as our only source of light. It was dim light, but sufficient for our purposes. I don't remember our trek down into the valley, or our exit, but we would have been following our daddy who would have been holding the lantern.

We fished from the west bank in a small pool of the creek's inky black water. I'm sure we were using our cane poles and I'm unsure what our bait was; probably we were using earthworms we had previously dug from near the shed where daddy had a small barrel with redworms in it that he periodically fed corn meal. We caught a lot of small, 6-8-inch catfish. These catfish populated the creeks near our home in abundance, and we, later, caught many of them without even baiting our hooks.

The next morning, my mother cooked those catfish in a frying pan and served them for our breakfast. I remember the sweet taste as I ate the meat right off the backbone. When I have the opportunity today, I prefer to have whole catfish rather than fillets. The taste is different and, I believe, much better. I had the opportunity to visit a catfish farm in central Arkansas that served a buffet featuring catfish taken that day (probably) from their large ponds. I first visited the buffet and took some catfish fillets, which were certainly very good, but later discovered, at the end of the buffet, a tray of large, whole catfish. I found them to be excellent with the taste I had remembered from earlier days.

Home Life

Christmas 1950 was our first Christmas in our Chapell Hill home. Our Christmas tree was a small cedar cut from one of the surrounding fields and, when brought into the house, infused it with the smell of cedar resin, a smell I have associated with Christmas since. The lights were a strand of sockets, cords, and multicolored lamps. To get the sockets to work, my daddy inserted match sticks in the socket bases at the cord entry points and, somehow, got these to hold in place and the lights to stay lit. It a wonder that cedar tree, and others to follow, didn't catch on fire, luckily, none of them did.

On Christmas Eve the lights were lit and left on for the night. Streaks of red and green and blue, and white, filtered through cracks between the bedroom door and its frame, and showed in widening streaks on the walls inside the bedroom creating a magical scene in anticipation of the next morning.

My present, that morning was a toy metal alligator, and I was delighted. It had a wind-up spring inside and, after having been wound and released, would run across the floor snapping its upper jaw while sparks flew out of its mouth. It was a good Christmas.

Before the next Christmas, the bedroom arrangements had been changed and I was sleeping in the other bedroom, which had a closet with an upper compartment closed by a hinged door. During the night, I was awake when my parents came in and took the presents out of that upper closet. I knew from then on, there was no Santa Claus. Christmas presents that year were mostly clothing, and I got some pajamas that had been ordered from a mail-order catalog, as did the other children.

Expanding Family

The bedroom sleeping arrangements had been changed because my mother had delivered her fifth child. This was my one, and only, sister, Ellen Kay; she was bedded in a new baby's crib. The family then consisted of my older brother, Royce Lee (by two years), myself, Jerry Thomas (I was seven at the time), then my next younger brother by four years Jimmy Charles, followed by Lanny Wade (two years younger, then Ellen. This birth order created grouping patterns among the children: there was my older brother, Royce, and I grouped together, then, as it worked out, the next three were grouped together; "Jimmy, Lanny and Ellen." Some years later, in 1957, my youngest brother, Timothy John, was a final surprise to the family.

My mother commented years later that her advice, when having children, was "Not to have one, by itself, but it was better to have two, and close together, so they could play and entertain each other." As busy as she was, that was probably well-learned advice. I remember "Jimmy, Lanny and Ellen" sitting in the floor, facing each together with their legs spread apart and rolling a ball between each other. That was probably a pretty good way to begin teaching them how to catch a ball that would later be thrown through the air.

The bedroom where my parents and now my sister slept was located over a cellar dug from the earth below. The dirt around the top sides of the cellar came up near the base of the house as served to restrict airflow from wind. That had the effect of allowing that bedroom to stay warmer during the winter nights due to the closed air space below. The other bedroom was higher from the ground on the "Pier and Beam" foundation and the cold air circulated freely under the floor. That made a considerable difference in the winter air temperatures at night in that room.

The sleeping arrangement was then changed again to put us four boys into the warmer bedroom and my parents and sister were in the other bedroom. This worked better because the room was larger, and the two double beds were necessary for us four boys to sleep. I was a bed-wetter, something over which I had no control, and my youngest brother also had the same problem. As a solution, the mattresses were encased in plastic and he and I were made to sleep in one bed and the other two brothers slept in the other bed. The mattresses were converted into innerspring mattresses by the Henshaw Mattress Company in Texarkana and were considered to be very good products.

"Pete" Carter

My paternal grandfather," Pete" Had been living alone in the rural home near Goodwater, Oklahoma. My grandmother, "Zona," had gone to Oregon. I'm sure that was an act of financial desperation. There she joined my Aunt Martha ("Marth-Ann," was how her name was spoken) who had gone there with her husband, "J.D." J.D. drove log trucks hauling logs out of the Cascade Mountains, and they lived in a small mountain town called "Sweet Home." That town lay close to the headwaters of the Santiam River.

Pete had a heart attack and was brought to the hospital in De Queen, where he stayed for a few days, then he was brought to stay in our home and placed in the bedroom where I had been sleeping. I don't remember what sleeping arrangements were made for us boys, but children can be very adaptable in those circumstances and, if we had a place to fall asleep, we were okay.

One day, on an afternoon, and into early evening, Pete began acting in a manner that frightened my mother and my aunt Mary Lou. All of us children were taken out of the house and onto the front porch, where we stayed until my daddy, who was somehow summoned to come home from his swing-shift job at the creosote treating plant, arrived to get the situation under control. When Daddy appeared, he aggressively indicated that all that concern was a ridiculous overreaction. Was it? Yes, or no, we went back into the house and Mama and my aunt no longer appeared to be fearful.

On a day, soon after that, I went into the bedroom and found my grandpa half-lying on the bed, where he had, apparently, tried to move from his chair to the bed and didn't make it. I went and reported this to my mother and aunt, and they investigated. I didn't know it, but he was dead. I knew something was amiss when my aunt began softly crying to herself.

The funeral was held in a cemetery in southeastern Oklahoma, not far from Goodwater where he had lived. I now know that place to be Philadelphia Cemetery. It was, at that time, located in a partially cleared area in a forest. Some native Indian graves were there and were notable by the small houses that had been built above the graves. My brother and I were instructed to stay inside the bed of the truck and not observe the ceremony and burial events. We did as we had been instructed.

I have since learned that, according to my mother, the man in the casket was not my grandpa. She said when she saw the body, she realized that person was not her father.

My grandmother, Zona, at first said she was not coming to the funeral, but then she decided she would, however, that required a four-day train ride from Oregon. The funeral home said they could not keep the body for that length of time and, it is alleged, they pulled a switcheroo with another body that came into their possession. Per my mother, it is most likely my grandpa was buried in an Idabel, Oklahoma cemetery. Records from that time would, most likely, be impossible to trace, making a search impractical. Later my grandmother was buried beside that grave with Pete Carter's name on it.

Pete Carter, incidentally, was not his real name either. He was Purley Melvin Cox from Tennessee. The spelling of "Purley" is what I have deduced to be the correct spelling, after the name of a small town in Tennessee near where his family lived. According to my mother who did a lot of genealogy investigation, his name is listed on a census as "Pearlie," which, I believe can't possibly be correct.

Story is that Purley enlisted in the Army and had served with the "Rough Riders" during the Spanish-American War under Teddy Roosevelt. Fearing that he would be sent to Panama when Malaria was prevalent and he would be under extreme risk, he deserted the Army, took the name of Carter, and headed west. In Wicks, Arkansas, he met my grandmother, Zona Mae Holt, who was about 14 at the time. They married and left for the oil fields of northern Oklahoma, where my mother, Thelma lea Carter, was born in Apperson, Oklahoma, a town which no longer exists today.

The Pig

The pig that had been brought from the Mt. Pleasant home to Chapel Hill. The farm had a much larger fenced pen that must have been at least a quarter of an acre, if not more, for the pig to live on. That pen was located under two white Oak trees at opposite corners and another oak tree stood in the middle of the pen. The shade produced by these trees was a large benefit to the pig.

The White Oak trees produce large acorns and one of them was situated near the northeast corner, but was, largely, outside the pen. One afternoon in the fall, the family was out under that tree; my daddy, for whatever reason, told my brother and me that he would pay us 5 Cents for each syrup bucket full of acorns we could gather from the ground and dump them in the pig's pen. My brother and I busily went about collecting the acorns and filling our buckets; we must have collected 3, or four, buckets-full before we had gathered almost all of them. Five cents were worth more back then than today, but considering our allowances were only a dime, (I'm not sure we were even getting allowances back then), this was good money.

A syrup bucket was a metal bucket, like a paint can, with a lid and a wire bail that held about a half-gallon of cane syrup, or molasses, when bought at the grocery store. Cans like these were always repurposed on the farm, and I'm sure they were also used for containers when we picked blackberries.

The pig was fed in a trough formed by joining two, approximately 10 inch wide, boards at a right angle along their length, then joining two end blocks in a manner that allowed the long boards to be held in a "V" and could hold the liquid slop that fed the pig. The "slop" was mixed using water in a five-gallon bucket, then mixing in a ration of "shorts," which was composed of fine bran particles, wheat germ and a small portion of floury endosperm particles that were, basically, white in color and dusty in texture. Other vegetable trimmings were provided as well.

Later, on the day "Pete" was buried, as my mother told me, a neighbor's dog had come by, invaded the pig pen, and killed our pig. To save the meat, the pig had to be processed and preserved right away. We came home from the funeral, I'm told, to find our neighbors in the process of slaughtering the pig. To accomplish this a frame of sorts was erected on the back of the smoke house. A rope and pulley were attached to the frame and a horsedrawn wagon's "singletree" was attached to the rope. The singletree was a sturdy wooden piece of harness used to attach the harness trace chains (the actual pulling linkage) to the fittings on a wagon. It had fittings on both ends that would have been attached to the harness trace chains, but in this case were used to hoist the pig for the final stages of slaughtering.

A barrel was tilted on its side and half buried in the ground for the first step in the slaughter process. Our pig was inserted into the hot water to loosen the hair on its body. The next step was scraping the hair to remove it. That job was assigned to me and my brother, and we eagerly set about accomplishing that using large knives held at 90-degree angles and scraping along the hide thusly pulling out the hair.

Gutting the pig was the next operation. The pig's rear legs, above the hooves, were attached to hooks on the ends of the single tree. The hooks were inserted through the legs between the Achilles tendon and the leg bones and provided a secure attachment to the single tree. The pig was hoisted by its rear legs and was ready for gutting.

The pig's belly was carefully slit open, and the guts spilled out into a washtub. To dispose of those, my brother and I were instructed to carry them, in the tub, down into the forest on a neighboring property and dump them there. The bowels would be disposed of by the scavengers of the forest, which included Turkey Vultures (we called them Buzzards). These large black birds, with long wings, could often be seen circling high up (about two hundred feet) in the sky. We knew when we saw them that something below them had died. At other times single birds could often be seen flying about the area, obviously searching for prey.

A collection of curing spices for preserving the meat was procured, the meat was coated with them and laid out in the smokehouse. There was never an effort to build and maintain a fire there and, I believe most of the meat was lost through spoilage. My mother told me later that she had made a lot of sausage using a hand-cranked grinder, but I don't know how that was preserved afterward. I don't remember having a lot of sausage at that time. We never raised another pig.

The Roof and Remodeling

During the early part of the summer when I was eight years old. (I believe I had completed the third grade) work had to be done on the roof of the house. The existing roof had been made of cedar shingles and was quite old when we had moved into the house. It was also necessary to build an additional room in the attic space to accommodate the larger family that the two bedrooms could no longer suffice.

The effort began with the removal of the shingle roof and the construction of a gable. That was necessary to house a lone window for the new upstairs bedroom, to be built later. The old shingles on the south portion of the roof were removed, and the remaining parts of an old kitchen brick chimney were dismantled brick-by-brick. The bricks were dislodged from the old mortar, which crumbled easily, then moved to a scaffold constructed at the edge of the roof before being tossed to the ground. I was tossing the bricks and my next younger brother, who was only four years old, was then picking them up and stacking them next to the house. There was a necessity to coordinate the tossing from the upper level and the pickup and stacking below. I was careful to toss only when the landing area was clear, however, after I made a toss, my younger brother suddenly emerged from under the scaffold and the brick narrowly missed his head. I was much more cautious when tossing the rest of the bricks.

The old shingle roof had been supported by spaced lateral slats that had six to eight-inch spaces between them. The new shingle roof needed solid surfaces to lay on, so new boards were fitted to fill the spaces between the previous slats. After the construction of the gable, the application of the new roof began, and my older brother and I became the roofing crew. Daddy crafted a device to cut the shingles on the angles necessary to fit them to the edges of the four main segments of the roof by using the back edge of a handsaw. It worked quite well. One morning, as I worked up on the roof, I wasn't wearing a shirt as it was a hot and humid day, a big red wasp landed in the middle of my back and stung me badly. It really hurt, but I continued with my work and the pain gradually dissipated.

After completing the gabled side of the roof, my brother and I moved to the east side and began by stripping off the old shingles, even down to the edges of the roof from which there was about a twelve-to-fourteen-foot drop to the ground. We did that without incident and completed that roof section by ourselves.

For the remaining two sections of roof, it was decided to leave the old shingles in place and, simply lay the new felt layer over them, then apply the shingles. That worked well and the work went along much faster until it was completed.

Later the "upstairs" bedroom was completed for the four of us boys to sleep in. My sister then had a downstairs bedroom alone. A stair section was created in an area of the previously existing parent's bedroom and a portion of the living room. The resulting stairs were steep with an ascent angle of, probably, close to sixty degrees from horizontal with very narrow steps that could only accommodate a climber's foot by standing sideways, or by having only the toes and ball of their foot on the stairsteps. These stairs worked well enough, and I don't know of anyone slipping and falling on them.

The flooring for this new upstairs room was made using four-inch-wide planed pine boards specially cut for this purpose with a groove along one side and a "tongue" on the other side. My brother and I were the ones who laid most of the flooring. It was not hard work, and we fitted the floor together quite well. The sides and ceiling of the room were constructed using pressed paper panels that I think came from the treating plant and had been used for the shipment of chemicals to the plant. It's quite possible those chemicals had permeated those panels. Nevertheless, those panels were used and, after installation, were painted blue with latex paint.

The gable provided a single window into the room, it also provided for a means of escape, in the event of a fire. A ladder was placed at the edge of the roof below the window for use in completing an escape. Inside the room, a railing made of pine two-by-fours covered two sides of the stair opening and the wall provided the covering of the third side. It was sturdy and worked quite well.

A clothes-hanging frame was made to hang our ironed shirts and pants, and a chest of four drawers, one for each boy and assigned from top to bottom according to age, was used for socks and underwear. A large oscillating fan helped to make sleeping possible during the summertime and, downstairs, a large window-sized exhaust fan drew outside air into the house and that helped greatly to make the summer nights more tolerable. During some summers, we sometimes moved our bed outside into the south yard and slept out in the cooler night air under the stars.

"Television"

The first time I ever saw a television, and the pictures it presented, was when I was ten years old. It was in the home of some relatives of a local family who had moved into the De Queen area from Weatherford, Texas. Our family was invited to their home on a Sunday afternoon and the show we saw was a dance/drama about "Billy the Kid:" the cowboy outlaw legend from New Mexico.

We subsequently got a TV set in our home; it was sited in a corner of the living room that had windows on both sides and the flat antenna wire lead-in was brought in beneath the window in its frame. The large antenna itself was positioned on the crest of the rooftop along a short ridge formed by the shingles my brother had installed previously. We got one channel, Channel 6 out of Texarkana, but that was plenty for us and I remember watching many cowboy films in the afternoon by some of the old stars like "Lash Larue" and others. The show was hosted by a TV personality called "Cowboy John" who always wore a cowboy hat during the show. "The Lone Ranger" and "Hopalong Cassidy" were other shows we saw and enjoyed - at least I did. Later shows like "Sing Along with Mitch Miller" starring Leslie Uggams and "The Grand Ole Opry," were favorites.

Previously to the TV, we had listened to the radio at night, and I specifically remember the "Lux Radio Theatre;" and other programs like "Amos and Andy," "The Great Gildersleeve," and "Sky King;" all of these fed the imagination of a young boy, which I was at the time.

"Thunder"

Shortly after we moved into the Chapel Hill home, the family made a trip to Grampa Pete's home in Oklahoma and brought back two young horses, a filly, and a colt. And, at first, placed them in the cow lot. My older brother and I, of course, attempted to ride them and did so without them having any harness, bridle, or saddle, at all. Now I realize how dangerous that really was, as we could have encounters with barbed wire on the tops of the fences, or even the low edges of the tin roof of the barn or could have been thrown into contact with other structures in the lot. A saddle and bridle had been brought from the farm, but we didn't think about using those in our eagerness to ride those horses. Those leather items were later determined to be dry and cracked in places, due to not having proper care with oils (linseed) rubbed into their surfaces at the proper times. The saddle was probably the one I had ridden in on the backwoods trip to the store with my grandmother.

Eventually, the filly was removed from our farm, and I had no idea where she was taken. That left the colt with us, and I was the one who most attempted to ride him. Daddy, at one time, attempted to "break" the colt for riding and had a rope on his head, but the colt was attempting to rear up on his hind legs and us his front feet to attack daddy, to free himself. At that point daddy got a large heavy wooden stick and used it to hit the young horse on his front legs when it reared up. Eventually that stopped and to my knowledge, was never done again.

Afterward, I would attempt to ride the colt, with some success, mostly bareback without a saddle and I had named him "Thunder." I remember riding him in the calf pasture without the saddle and being thrown up onto his neck, before being thrown onto the ground. Luckily the pasture was covered with grass and the soil beneath was soft and I sustained no injuries. I, however, persisted with my riding attempts and felt that he was my horse.

Later in the summer, a nearby teenage girl whose family had horses, one of those being an older filly, suggested she and I go riding early one morning. The filly's name was "Sugar" and a mare, named "Dolly," was her mother. I had often ridden Dolly, who, upon command, would rear up on her hind legs much like "Roy Rogers" (cowboy film star) would do in his films.

On the appointed morning, I rose early and, although I don't fully remember what transpired, I got Thunder and went for the ride. Afterward, my mother gently told me that I was not to be doing that sort of thing without letting her and my daddy know what was planned. That instruction was all that was needed and there was never any future problem.

Not long after the ride, it became noticeable that Thunder's hooves had grown and were splitting along the edges. Daddy made some effort to trim the hooves but couldn't give them the care they needed. One morning, without any prior discussion, Daddy saddled him and rode off to take him to the sale barn, where livestock were auctioned off to the highest bidder. We didn't have the means to transport him by trailer and he was too big to be transported by riding in the bed of the pickup truck with the removable sideboards my daddy had built to attach to the bed. Those sideboards made it useable for hauling cows when needed. So, he set out on the ride, which was probably about five miles total. I found out later that Thunder wasn't, in the end, taken to the sale barn, because someone saw him and my daddy on the road and bought the young horse right there. That was the end of "Thunder."

The Chickens

Not long after we had arrived in Chapel Hill, in the winter of the new year, the family started to make use of the two chicken houses on the property. The smaller of the two houses was a brooder house where baby chicks were started and would live until they were ready to start laying eggs. The other house was a laying house that was set up with a honeycomb-like arrangement of dry grass lined "nests" where hens would lay their eggs, and a roost that was a gradually sloping arrangement of long poles positioned horizontally, where they would spend the nights sitting on the poles with their talons wrapped around the poles.

The brooder house was prepared for the baby chicks with new wood shavings spread on the floor and a sheet metal, broad, cone-shaped brooder that was placed under an electrical connection on the ceiling. The brooder was designed to use a kerosene burner to provide heat, but in lieu of that, an electrical heat lamp using a single high-wattage and red-colored bulb was suspended over the large hole in the middle top of the metal cone.

The baby chicks arrived in a large three-foot square box that was about six inches in depth, with holes in the sides for air ventilation. These were picked up at the post office and, as I later found out, had been shipped by train from Kansas City.

One by one, the chicks were picked up out of the box, their beaks were dipped in some water (there was no water in the shipping box) then placed in the brooder. Several food trays filled with special chick feed had been placed under the brooder, along with watering bottles and bowls. The food trays were about a foot long, with a row of round holes on each side of the ridged top. The watering bottles were capped by a special round bowl that fitted to the tops of the bottles. These were inverted and placed on the floor of the brooder. The water level in the trays was controlled by the amount of air allowed in the bottles. When the level dropped below the rim of the bottle, air would be drawn into the bottle, but once an amount of water was drained into the bowl, the rim of the bottle was sealed and no more water could escape, thus, the water level was maintained in the trays until the bottles were empty.

This was all in the winter and the temperatures were cold at night and warmer during the days. The windows of the brooder house were made with sheets of bubble plastic and allowed sunlight to come in during the day, which helped to warm the house, but then the temperatures dropped at night. As the temperatures varied it was necessary to vary the height of the heat lamp as it had to be lowered during the nights and raised during the days. Keeping the lamps at the proper height was, of course, an inexact science, done mostly by trial-and-error, and frequent adjustments.

With the heat lamp raised and the temperatures falling, the chicks would be found huddled directly under the lamp and it had to be lowered to provide more heat inside the brooder. Later, when temperatures had risen, the chicks would be found dispersed to the outside edges of the brooder and the lamp had to be raised. The cycle was then repeated each day. I remember mostly taking care of the lamp positioning myself when I was home.

The young chicks grew and developed into young poulet's (females) and cockerels (males). The cockerels (I didn't know that word until many years later) were eventually separated and became food for the family. One was kept, he was allowed to become a rooster and the flock was his.

Later, when the poulets grew into young hens, they were moved into the laying house where they eventually began laying eggs. At first the eggs were small and resembled eggs from songbirds, then the larger eggs started coming. Some of these eggs from these young hens contained two yolks and were, of course, oversized, or "jumbo," eggs, as they are sold today. I buy those jumbo eggs when I can find them, and some of those are, occasionally, "double-yolkers," which I know came from young hens.

The Garden

AS mentioned previously, the garden was on a fenced plot about ¾'s of an acre in size. In the northwest corner was a section of plowed ground that provided the soil for rows of vegetables. The early plantings were "English Peas," which are like "Sugar Snaps," or "Snow Peas," except the husks were uneatable, especially when we harvested them. These provided the first fresh vegetables, with green spinach coming after them.

Later in the spring, the onions and tomatoes, which were purchased in bundles of very small plants, were planted in a one-by-one fashion: a finger-sized hole (actually formed using a finger) was punched in the soil, then a little water was poured into the hole (to give the plant roots a good start) just before inserting the plant and compressing the soil around the roots.

A large, probably 50-pound, sack of potatoes was purchased for planting a new crop. Whole potatoes were cut into segments, with each segment containing an "eye." A furrow would be cut into the ground, then potato segments would be dropped into the furrow, before plowing the dirt back into the furrow. When the potatoes were harvested, they were taken under the back (raised) portion of the house and spread out on the ground there. We then spread lime on the potatoes, which acted as a preservative and kept them usable until the next crop could be harvested.

Beans of several varieties would be planted as well; these would be "Purple Hull," "Crowder," or "Black-eyed" peas," and "Pinto" and green "Snap" beans. The sweet corn was planted in several rows on the south side of the vegetable patch, but in that area, there were roots of "Johnson Grass," that was (for us) impossible to eradicate. As I recall the corn from that area was never good and the yields were small.

To the east of the two pecan trees, lay a small patch of ground that was often used for tomatoes. I always really disliked the smell of those tomato vines then and still don't to this day. One year that patch was prepared in the late summer for a crop of turnips, which are a "fall" crop, instead of a spring crop. The area was plowed and harrowed to being nearly smooth then the turnip seeds were broadcasted over the area. Care was taken that the planting occurs on the 14th of August, which was, according to local lore, the ideal date for turnips. I don't recall a good harvest, and I don't know what we would have done with the turnips had we successfully grown a lot of them.

In a corner near the turnip patch was a small sunken area protected by sideboards and a clear plastic cover. This was a "hotbed" created by the previous owners and would have been used for starting plants from seeds early in the spring for transplanting out into the garden later, but we never used it at all. One highly unusual thing about this area was that Poppies voluntarily grew there for years. These were beautiful plants with silvery stalks and gorgeous flowers. The seed pods formed after the blooms and, I guess, could have contained the raw tar that could be processed in heroin, but we didn't know anything about that.

The second year for the garden, my daddy decided to grow peanuts on the unbroken pastureland south of the garden. That patch of land had a single small tree standing on it. I believe it was pear tree, but it had no pears that I know of. The ground was tilled and planted and once, I believe, we were sent to hoe the weeds out of it.

The soil, however, was very poor in nutrients and yielded very small amounts of very small peanuts per stalk. These stalks were gathered up and placed in the brooder chicken house for drying. Once dry, we could strip the peanuts off the stalks and eat them. We never raised any more peanuts on the farm.

The garden was an important source of food for the large family and much of the produce was preserved by canning or packaged for freezing in the chest freezer we acquired later.

Third Grade

I don't remember much about the time I spent in the third grade, but I do remember having Mrs. Prince as our teacher. She was a kindly woman, seemingly very pretty and well dressed. Her husband was the owner of the local Prince's Hardware store, and they had a weekend cottage that had been built on stilts on land near the Rolling Fork River near the Hwy 70 bridge mentioned earlier. Their city home was located on the street corner on the northwest side of the Central Elementary School grounds. I'm sure that made her commute very convenient. Another teacher, Mrs. Horne, lived even closer, having a home in the middle of the block directly across the street from the school.

In class, several of us began working ahead on our in-class-completed math assignments by doing the next day's assignments, for which we had no instruction, during the time we were given to work on that day's assignment. I don't know who started that practice, but I know it wasn't me. I think one of the principal instigators went on later to achieve a degree in chemistry and worked as a chemist for his lifelong career.

In The Garden

Somewhere during this time, I was in the garden by the garden tractor, and I may have been putting oil in the engine, when my daddy walked up to me and said, "You're the most sissy one of the bunch!" What does one, especially a child, do to deal with that? All I could do, and did do, was to inure myself, as best I could, against his hate. I never said anything to anyone about It, until in recent years. Before she passed, I told my mother. She said something interesting at that time, which was a summation of those years. She said he was jealous of me, that I was everything he wanted to be. I don't think he wanted to be a sissy, as he labeled me at that time, but in the later teen years, when more trouble came, I could see where that possibly could be true. I will add that later, in high school, I was the one who seriously participated in football, and I won recognition and rewards from it. My daddy never acknowledged any of that and seemed insulted by it all.

Mr. Turner's Farm

One of my first jobs was helping to harvest red radishes from Mr. Turner's field. In the early part of the year, he had planted small red radishes on a three-acre (about) field to the west of his home: they had grown in the cool weather, and he needed them to be harvested. The way this was done was for the workers; his daughter, me and my older brother, and maybe others, to work on our hands and knees to gather the radishes in our hands. We would gather up a good handful by pulling them out of the ground by their green tops, then put a rubber band around the bundle and toss them into a container, which was probably a bushel basket. We probably worked a couple of days to complete the harvest. I seem to remember that his daughter bought some "Toreador" pants with her earnings.

Mr. Turner also had a strawberry patch on a hillside on the north side of his property. The hillside soil was mostly gravel which is good for growing strawberries, and for several years, in the spring, my brother and I picked them. We did this by taking a wooden hand-held carrier, filling it with six thin wood quart boxes and then filling those boxes with ripe strawberries as we worked our way along the hillside rows. Much of the work was on our hands and knees, but we were glad to get the work (and the pay) and we picked until the harvest was complete.

Mr. Turner worked his farm with horses only and had the older mare "Dolly," that I mentioned before she was a stocky animal and had some draft horse lineage in her bloodline, I'm sure. One day I saw her after she had been working for some time in the field; she had a raw place on her left hindquarters where the harness used to attach to whatever implement she had been pulling, had been rubbing against her skin. This does not imply that she was in any way mistreated by Mr. Turner and I'm sure the work wasn't stopped due to the necessity of getting it completed. She would have been, subsequently, treated and the spot left to heal.

He worked on his farm very diligently and, among other things, grew corn, mostly to feed his animals. He had a tool in an outbuilding that would, in a single operation, strip all the kernels off a dried ear of corn and toss the stripped cob out the top of the machine. I thought it was wonderful, and still do, but there were many implements of this nature at that time that were mechanical marvels and saved a lot of manual labor.

We had another family that lived just across the road from the Turners: the Wrights. I didn't have much interaction with them, except that I was outside with him in his toolshed, and he handed me a Japanese soldier's rifle bayonet and the sheath it had with it. His son had collected these items during the war and, apparently, he didn't want this one. I took the bayonet home and played with it occasionally to mainly find out its characteristics. My mother told me that, after I left home, she found it, was quite alarmed and took it to the old chicken house and hid it high up on a ledge near the roof.

At one point in time our family was buying milk from the Turners: it was supplied in milk bottles that had compressed paper tops, like the old-style milk bottles that used to be delivered to city houses daily. I was sent to return the used bottles and pick up the newly filled bottles. I decided to experiment with the strength of the stopper and turned one bottle upside down. Well, I found out that the stopper wasn't all that secure as it came loose and spilled the milk onto the road. I think I had to take the bottle back and get a refill; lesson learned.

Fourth Grade

For some reason the design of the school's classrooms comes to mind when I think of the fourth grade. The school did not have air conditioning at that time but had been designed to have windows that opened at both the top and bottom so that both could be opened and let convection air flow cool the rooms as best it could. The hotter air near the ceilings would exit the top through the window openings and the cooler(?) air could enter through the open bottom windows. The window arrangement seemed adequate for the time, and we made the best of the situation. I don't remember being uncomfortable in the classrooms.

In my classroom, one of the students was subject to having epileptic seizures. He had been in another classroom before this year and had before been with some of the students in my classroom. The first time one of the seizures occurred, the students from his previous class all rose and filed out of the classroom to an outside area. I saw this happening and I rose and filed out with the rest of the class. When we came back, our teacher asked what that was all about and instructed us that, should it happen again, we were to remain in our seats.

That year was our introduction to music and were instructed on the playing of a "Tonette;" some might call it a "Sweet Potato" and that's what it looked like. I enjoyed playing it and thought it was fun. Later, I understand the "recorder" became the instrument of choice for student's introduction to music.

My younger brother, who was more than four years younger than me, started school that year. He was only 5 at the time, but, because his birthday was before the year ended, he was enrolled in school. One afternoon my mother instructed me to take him to the restroom and show him how to use it. The next day I was presented with a problem: If I obeyed my mother, I would be violating school rules as, being a fourth grader, I wasn't allowed to go down the hall by the first and second grade classrooms. I chose to follow the immediate authority I had to face. Later, in the afternoon, a teacher appeared at the door to my classroom, and I was called out. I was told to take care of my little brother, and he was given to me. No further instructions or suggestions were given. He had been unable to hold back his bowels and had messed in his pants in the classroom.

All I could think of was to take him outside onto the playground while we waited for the school bus to take us home. Some of the excrement rolled out of his pants onto the ground and was left there. We were able to mount the bus and make the ride to where we got off the bus, some of the other kids saw the stains on the rear of his pants and, of course, exclaimed that everyone should look.

When we got home, my mother was extremely upset and between her getting my brother cleaned up and cooking supper, found time to get a peach tree switch (I think I actually had to go and cut it from the tree) and she gave me a whipping. The next day I violated school rules and took my brother to the restroom and showed him how to use it. Years later I told my mother I had been put in a quandary by her directive and the school rules. She said she had wondered about that for forty years. That didn't make a difference however, as the damage had been done. One of the lasting effects of this was that there was some build-up of resentment on my part toward my younger brother and that would create some problems.

Hauling Hay

In the summers it was necessary to replenish the stock of hay bales in the barn used for feeding the livestock during the winters. My daddy would use the pickup and load many bales in a stacked fashion that I thought would have exceeded the capacity of that half-ton truck. He would start by filling the small bed with maybe six bales, then add the next layer by positioning the added ones partially overhanging both sides of the bed. That pattern was repeated for two more layers, then a centered single row was added on top. All of this was secured by a single rope across the top row and down to the rear bumper. It seemed to work well and didn't exceed the capacity of the truck, except for once.

On a summer's day my brother and I went with him to a field on the north side of the river north of highway 70. The field was clearly in an area that was occasionally flooded over by the river and had rolling contours where water had eroded the surface of the land. The vegetation in the field was also, not all grass, which left some cut off stalks ("stobs" is what we called them) of large weeds standing on the surface of the soil. These stobs were quite sturdy and presented a hazard in many ways.

We were in the process of gathering and loading the bales, when the right tire on the back of the pickup was punctured by a stob, blew out and went flat. The tire was one of the "mud grips" and had worn thin in the center of the tread. My brother and I, of course, got involved in trying to change the tire. The screw-action jack was successfully positioned under the axel and cranked to move the truck up off the tire. I think we had the tire removed when the truck rolled forward and fell off the jack. I realized in later years that I had been sitting with my foot under the truck near where the tire had been. If that fall had happened at that time, my ankle would have been crushed. Luckily, that didn't happen.

Each summer we hauled hay from various fields around the area and stored the bales in the barn. Each bale had to be moved, lifted, and stacked and there were probably at least one hundred bales. The stack in the barn was probably eight bales high and had to be arranged so that the bales could be accessed from the inside door of the barn but was moved in and stacked from the rear door. That barn wasn't well-made and, except for the hay storage area, had only dirt for a floor, and that got wet and mired in the winter. The main parts of the barn were built using old four-cylinder automobile engine blocks set on rocks as a foundation.

During the winter, the hay was given out in partial bales called "blocks," which were bale divisions about three inches wide formed when the bailer compressed the grass taken in from the field with one stroke of the compressing mechanism. A milk cow was given two blocks of hay each day, along with a ration of grain-based feed. It all worked well, and I did a lot of cow milking when I was there.

Squirrel Hunting

The only hunting we did, as a family and separately, was for squirrels, mostly what my daddy called Fox Squirrels, which are brown with reddish orange undersides, and, occasionally, grey squirrels. Daddy had a single shot, bolt action Winchester .22 caliber rifle that he had acquired as a youth. It was a very good rifle and was very accurate, if aimed correctly.

On one cold November morning, he and my brother and I went hunting in the woods north of the highway on land that led down to the river bottom land of Rolling Fork; I was probably eight years old at the time. After a while, I got very cold; my feet were cold, my ears were cold, and I was miserable. I didn't complain however and carried on, while noting that wearing two pairs of socks might be a pretty good idea. I don't think we got any squirrels that day either.

Later, daddy bought a Mossberg 20 Gauge shotgun that had a variable choke on the end of the barrel and a magazine that held two, or three, extra shells. It had a bolt action loading system and, all-in-all, was an ungainly looking piece that was heavy for its gauge. I never remember daddy using that shotgun on any of our hunts. After a while, that shotgun disappeared from our home.

One of my daddy's favorite activities was to go squirrel hunting on Christmas Eve and take all of us boys along. He always had that day off from his work and always organized the hunt. Sometimes, one of us would be carrying a BB rifle; that didn't matter because we were "hunting." I came to enjoy these hunts, and, for me, that was some of the magic of Christmas; it certainly kept us occupied for that afternoon.

In my high school years (I think I was a sophomore), a 410 Gauge Winchester shotgun was acquired and, somehow, that became my designated gun. It was a good quality piece, and it had obviously been well used by the previous owner, but it had one problem: the shell ejector lip was broken, making removal of the shells after firing, or just unloading the weapon difficult. But I was still glad to have it and pleased that it was designated as mine. A new single shot 12 Gauge shotgun was purchased after the 410 was acquired. It was an Iver-Johnson break-open piece that had a long thin barrel. It was, comparatively, light in weight and easy to carry in the woods. It's light weight, however, made it give more recoil, or "kick," when it was fired.

We had a female dog that was a long-haired mix resembling an English Spaniel, her name was "Lucky," because she had been the only one kept out of her litter; I don't know what happened to the others. She accompanied us on hunts and was useful in locating squirrels, but she also would go off into the woods close to our house and hunt on her own. Many times, we heard her barking in a voice and pattern that let us know she had "treed" a squirrel. On one day she had one treed and I grabbed a couple of shells for the 410 and went down into the woods to find the dog.

Shortly after following a cow's trail across a small stream, I found her and located the squirrel in the tree she was barking at. I slipped a shell into the chamber of the 410, aimed and took the shot. When the shot hit the squirrel, it flew sideways off the tree and onto the ground. When I examined it, I found there were several large holes in its body that were inconsistent with the No. 6 shot that was supposed to be in the shell. Then I remembered that, earlier on, my daddy had opened one of those shells and replaced the No. 6 shot with .00 buckshot from one of his 12-gauge shells. A 410 shotgun shoots just as hard as a 12 gauge but has a smaller load of shot pellets.

The squirrel had to be taken home, skinned, and dressed and was supposed to be meat for the family to eat. The few times we ever had squirrels, I never liked it.

Usually it was fried, but that was tough and barely edible; squirrel and dumplings was another way of preparing it, but that wasn't any better in my opinion.

48 Ford

During the second year, or third year in Chapel Hill, it was, apparently, decided that the family needed another automobile. Having only the pickup and Daddy driving that to his work left Mom at home with five children and no means of purchasing needed supplies and, more importantly, being able to transport the children to receive emergency care, should that arise.

A trip was arranged to Texarkana to shop for a used car; there a two-door 48 Ford sedan was found and purchased. The salesman accompanied my daddy to a bank there to complete the financial arrangements.

As we were using the car, a seating patten developed that had my older brother sitting on the right outside, I sat on the left outside behind the driver and the two younger brothers sat in the middle. As I would get into the back seat, I would place my hand on the car door frame to help move into my seat. My daddy always drove the car and five or six times he closed the door while my hand was still on the door frame. Luckily, my fingernails were never caught by the closing door and there was enough of a gap between the door and the frame, (remember this was a Ford) that my fingers were only slightly mashed, without any lasting damage. One would think that after a couple of times a parent would remember and start checking before closing the car door.

When the family drove the car on trips over into Oklahoma, on the return trips, typically on a Sunday afternoon, my mother would tune the radio (this car had one - a first for us) to the Wittnauer Music Hour which played classical music concerts.

I liked listening and I think that influenced my musical preferences later.

The two-door Ford was, eventually, traded in on a "49" Chevrolet four-door Deluxe sedan, which was a much nicer car and better accommodated the family.

The Band

In the Fifth grade in elementary school, it was possible to begin instrumental music training. I began the training and was directed to begin learning to play the baritone tuba. I didn't know it was a tuba, I just knew it as a baritone, and I liked its sound.

My older brother had previously begun band training and was given a brand-new coronet horn to play, which is, of course, a much smaller instrument and it had a smaller mouthpiece than the tuba. I was required to rent the baritone for about $2.50 a month from the school.

All my Fifth-Grade year I played the baritone in the junior band, and, of course, playing in a marching band was part of curriculum. We were given uniforms, that must have been a sight to see, and we traveled to a Nashville Junior high school game on a bus and marched and played at halftime. I remember doing a reversing movement where the band was marching toward the end zone of the football field when row-by-row we would turn to the side and begin marching in the opposite direction back toward the middle of the field.

I liked the music, and I liked the overtures we played in the spring. Learning to read music (somewhat) was helpful in later years. In the spring the band was to play in a competition of school bands from our region that was held in Hope, Arkansas. Both my older brother and I were to participate in our respective groups and the bands were to be transported by school buses to that event. For some reason that I never understood, my mother drove us to Hope in our car and all the children were brought along. We had lunch in a city park where some play rides, such as swings and a self-powered merry-go round were available.

There was a problem that developed, however, from playing the baritone. The mouthpiece was very large and too large for my mouth. The skin below my lips became chapped during the spring. I kept putting Vaseline on it; so that helped a little as I finished the year in the band.

In the sixth grade, our band practice was held during the school lunch hour and the band members were transported by bus over to the band hall at the high school (when were we supposed to eat lunch?). There was a major problem, however, with playing in the band and what I really wanted to do. Lunchtime was the period when the boys on the playground gathered to play football on the northwest side of the school in an area that was covered in large gravel rocks. We chose up sides and played tackle football. Many times, my hands were bloodied in spots where the skin was badly scraped from bracing myself against falling to the ground. One boy, whose name that we knew as "Butch," lived nearby to the school brought his football for us to play our games.

Playing in the band prevented me from playing in the noon football games. There were two tracks for boys in junior high and high school: one was band, the other was athletic sports: football, basketball and running track. The practice times for the band, and all the sports, especially in high school, were the Last Period of the school day. The band was also the marching band for football games. Clearly, one couldn't do both, but one person did by playing football in the fall, then playing in the band for the rest of the school year.

There was also an issue with paying the band dues; my mother gave me a check that had been written to her by a third party. She endorsed the check and gave it to me to pay the band dues, which I did. Well, there was an issue with that with the school and I was called in to the office to explain the check. I believe they went ahead and processed the check, as I heard nothing further from it.

I started skipping band practice to go play football, and was, eventually, called into the office to explain. As a result, I was no longer in the band. At home this was discussed at the dinner table, where my daddy instantly said: "You're a Quitter!" This was completely without any effort, or apparent thought, to try to understand my reasoning or desires. I just sat there at the table and said nothing; there would have been no use and only additional humiliations would have been ensuing. There were never, ever, any thoughts considered other than his own before he made his instant judgements and proclamations.

The Fifth Grade

Mrs. King was my teacher that year, and the year in class was not particularly notable, but there were a few significant things that stood out in my memory. The first of these is that, prior to the start of the year, at home there was some discussion of clothing provisions to be made for the year. At one point my daddy looked at me and said, "You will wear overalls!" There was no discussion of what I would like, or would have chosen, or if that was the standard for the family (it wasn't). It was just a point-blank arbitrary decision that, quite frankly, I suspect, may have been made because he knew I didn't like overalls; they weren't the clothing norm and I hadn't worn them in the past, nor had any of the other children. He meant to humiliate me and evidence his power over me.

The rest of the school year, I wore overalls and that was a source of constant embarrassment for me. I wore my shirts on the outside every day to, at least partially, cover up the overalls.

That year, the father of one of my classmates, who taught math courses in high school, came to our classroom several times to conduct an experiential learning exercise by introducing us to the concepts of Algebra. I thought it was interesting and quickly grasped those concepts. After a few sessions, the experiment ended.

I was introduced to the use of a telephone that year and those of us who didn't have a telephone in our home were, one by one, taken into the office and were instructed to talk on the phone with one of the teachers; she lived across the street from the school and had a daughter in my class. I remember the sound being somewhat mechanical, but I clearly recognized her voice.

There was also some boyfriend/girlfriend activity in the classroom and there was a girl I was loosely associated with. I mention this because, the next, and subsequent years, she was no longer in the class, but she did reappear some years later, under some odd circumstances.

Another event happened in the Chapel Hill Community about this year. It was during the summer and one of the neighbor boys, who my older brother and I knew casually, drowned while swimming across a creek. I was told it was because of him getting caught up in some underbrush in that creek. Our daddy determined that, as a lesson for us, we were to attend the funeral. It was in the Wilkerson funeral home there in De Queen and I remember very little about the service, except being uncomfortable sitting on the hard wooden benches. We sat through the service and left. I guess the message I retained was that there can be unintended consequences for some things, but beyond that, what else?

The Pond

About the third year that we lived in the Chapel Hill house, it was decided/arranged to have a large (approximately one acre) stock pond dug in the larger cow pasture. I think it was a U.S. Government USDA program that helped upgrade the land. The spot chosen for the pond was where a pre-existing small, manually dug, pond existed. It was the natural low point of the pasture, and all excess rainwater drained there, plus there was a small creek from the neighboring land that emptied into the area as well.

The dozer cut into the yellowish red earth and dug deeper and deeper tracks from the north to the south, piling it along a fence line along the south side of the pasture that formed the farm's boundary. The result was a new hole in the earth that, when filled with water, would form about a half-acre water surface area pond that would be about 10 feet deep at the lowest point. Certainly, that would be enough for our small herd of cows.

The dam was formed with an east-to-west flat upper surface, that was about the width of a dozer blade. The height was about six feet above the land surface. Of course, all of this was bare, and loosely packed earth.

Shortly after the digging was completed and during a rainstorm with lightning bolts and thunder occurring, my daddy got us out and had us gather Bermuda Grass roots and runners from a garden area that had mostly been used for growing watermelons. We took the roots and runners and made them sprigs for planting on the bare earth of the dam. We spread the sprigs on the loose bare earth and pressed them in with our feet. This was done to help stop the erosion of the earth that formed the dam and save it from being washed back into the pond area. Of course, the few sprigs we planted only helped in the longer term and really did nothing to stop the effects of the on-goings storm. The dam eventually was covered with grass and has lasted to this day.

Later, when the pond filled with runoff water, it became a swimming hole for us and my older brother and I even constructed a diving board, of sorts. Oddly, when thinking about this, I think when we chose the shallow side of the pond, rather than the deeper side off the dam, we erred in our judgement and could have had a better platform.

To bring the pond to life and begin the fish population, all four of us brothers would take our fishing poles and go to the creek in Mr. Wight's pasture carrying a bucket. We would take the small sun perch, bream, and catfish we caught and place them in the water in the bucket. We then carried the bucket of fish back to the pond and poured them into the water. We repeated this several times and it must have worked because we later caught some of those fish, particularly on a flyrod with a small fly white lure. We never caught any catfish, but we never really fished in a way that would get them to bite either. I'm sure there were some big mudcats laying in the bottom of that pond.

At one time, we caught a very large (about fourteen inches across its shell) alligator snapping turtle (which was as ugly as that prehistoric animal could be) on the shallow side of the pond. I don't know how, or why, that turtle got into our pond, because there was no real stream of water connecting to the pond, either coming or going.

We later swam in the pond and were encouraged by my mother to go swimming in the early morning before breakfast. I don't know if we did that more than a couple of times and mostly swam in the afternoons when we needed some outside activities. I would go out into the middle of the pond at its deepest point and submerge in a vertical fashion by using my extended arms in an upward motion sending me downward to the bottom of the pond. The bottom was probably about eight feet deep at point. I never felt there was any problem with my safety while doing this, of course I was just a kid at the time, but I was a good swimmer and could easily do all of this.

My daddy, later, got some used clothing from somewhere and gave me a pair of red shorts to wear as a swimsuit. Those shorts turned out to have been made for girls and, of course, they didn't fit right, but that didn't matter to him, and that's all I had to wear swimming.

The Softball Team

The summer when I was 10 years old, and turning 11 in August, the management of the creosote plant organized a softball league, which played their games at the local county fairgrounds. As it turned out, for many of the games, not enough players showed up to make a full team. As a result, my older brother and I were allowed to play in many of the games to field a full team; I thought that was great!

At a game in the not-too-distant town of Dierks: named for the company's (Dierks Forests Inc.) mill there; again, not enough players showed up and I got to play. I was playing in the infield at second base when the other team's batter hit a high pop fly in my direction. As I tried to catch the ball, I had to look upward into the night sky beyond the lights. As I did so, I lost perspective of the ground and, consequently, was unable to determine the speed and path of the ball. Another regular player was off to my right, but he didn't try to intervene; as a result, I didn't make the catch, and the ball fell a few yards behind me. A similar situation occurred years later when I was playing in a men's industrial league in Oregon; I was playing Right Field when a very high pop fly was hit up almost beyond the lights, with similar results. Apparently, it takes some training and experience to properly make that play.

The last game was played back at the fairgrounds, and I was playing again. The game wound down and I was the last batter. Whether I got a hit, or not, would determine the winner of the game. I got the pitch coming in toward me and swung at it, hitting the ball down the first baseline. The player there, who was the father of one of the girls in my school class, was apparently surprised at the hit and, although the ball hit his glove, he failed to catch it, giving me a hit. The base runner ahead of me scored and we won the game.

Oregon

During the summer of '54, the family ventured to travel to Oregon where my grandmother Zona Lived in the small Cascades Forest logging town of Sweet Home (mentioned previously). We left out in our 1949 Chevrolet and first traveled west to spend the night in Lawton Oklahoma where my daddy's sister Maxine lived with her Husband Bill.

On the way we came upon Lake Texoma, which is a large Corps of Engineers flood control lake on the boundary between Texas and Oklahoma. My older brother and I had never seen such a massive amount of water and were amazed at its immensity. Mom commented on our amazement "Well, just wait until they see the ocean." The ocean was not, however, particularly remarkable to us when we saw it.

Toward the end of that first day we drove on, into the early evening, until we reached our destination. We had not eaten for quite a while before we arrived and during those final hours my stomach began to be increasingly painful. I said nothing and endured the pain until we were fed later.

The next day we traveled into Colorado and made it into Pueblo where we stopped for the night and, after checking several motels, found one and stopped for the night. The next day we headed off into the Rocky Mountains following the Arkansas River where we found a roadside picnic area on the river and stopped to cook breakfast.

A wood fire was built, and Mom began cooking breakfast in an iron skillet. As our breakfast was being prepared, my older brother and I took out his bait casting rod and reel and began casting a big heavy "spoon" lure, out into the rapidly flowing water. We thought we were getting "bites," but the lure was just bumping on the rocky bottom and semi-snagging on the rocks. Anyway, we were actively engaged, and our breakfast was soon ready. I'm sure the fried bacon and eggs tasted great!

Later, we drove our way deeper into the mountains and were soon climbing up Monarch Pass with our car in a lower gear as we climbed the final grades up to the summit. There we stopped, and, while walking around, immediately noticed the thin air that caused us to breathe rapidly. The view was, of course, amazing. I would love to visit that place again and relive that experience.

A lot of the rest of the trip is a blur in my memory, but I do remember the high desert between Burns and Bend, Oregon, and the sage colored vegetation along the roadsides.

In Sweet Home, my grandmother lived in an apartment complex where the only bathing facility was a shared area set off in a separate building, but, just outside, there was a cherry tree nearby full of ripe red cherries, and a small stream flowed at the edge of the compound. My older brother and I spent a lot of time in that creek and built several dams using the stones we found there. We all stayed in that apartment, which seemed to have a large open living area where we could all find a place to sleep.

We drove, with my grandmother, one day to the Oregon Pacific Coast, which we found to be cold and windy. I noticed the heather-like vegetation growing on the hills just before the beach and the stiff wind blowing in from the ocean. After descending to the water, we found some large driftwood trees laying on the flat sandy beach and stayed near them for a while; the driftwood providing some semi-protection from the wind.

We later drove down the coastline to Depot Bay, where we saw the fishing boats that use that protected bay, and the harbor seals that live there. The bay has a narrow entrance from the ocean with massive rocks on each side. The boats slowly motor through this passage while swaying heavily in the crossing waves of the ocean. Later in life, I would revisit the bay and even take a boat cruise down the coastline to a protected cove populated by a few seals on its sandy beach. On the return trip from the cove, the captain allowed the children to climb onto the top of the cabin where the swaying of the boat would be amplified over what was experienced on the lower deck; apparently this was something the children enjoyed often.

On an afternoon we all went to the city park and, once there, went swimming in the park pool. The water was a shock to me because it was cold. I had only swum in the warmer waters of the rivers around my home and thought they were cool at times. Those river waters also felt cool to me because of the warm-to-hot temperatures of the surrounding air.

Near the city park pool, we found some gymnastic equipment including some Olympic style "Still Rings." I didn't know that was what they were, and I gave them a try. I abandoned the effort quickly after finding them unpleasant.

On one day a gentleman friend of my grandmother's came by and offered to take one of us to the movie in town that afternoon. For some reason, I was chosen; why? I don't know. When I returned Home, I was relieved that I was no longer with a stranger. On another day, in the morning, I was taken to the local telephone switching center with my grandmother and saw her performing her job cleaning the floor under the switching equipment frames. I would learn a lot more about that equipment when I worked with Southwestern Bell Telephone many years later. I have the impression that one of the reasons I was asked to go along to these events was to give me some time away from Daddy to the extent they could. My grandmother would have been very sensitive to my situation and surely, she and my mother would have talked.

My mother told me, years later, that, when I was young, I had a head full of black hair (and green eyes that my mother said looked like jewels). My daddy said I was different from the others, and he questioned whether, or not, I was even one of his children. I believe the black hair and eyes were inherited from my mother's father who came from Tennessee where, I have learned, such traits are more common. My older brother has said that I look like Grandpa Pete.

The Trip Home

Our route took us south through Oregon and into Northern California where we saw the giant Sequoia Trees in the redwood forest. We stopped for a while and marveled at their size and the road built through the base of one.

Later we reached Southern California and saw a small, very unusual, building beside the road that was shaped like an orange. We stopped and were treated to an Orange Julius. It was, as best I remember, very, very, good. Haven't ever had another one.

The next day we were on our way across Arizona (in July). To help us, we used washcloths soaked in water and held over the window air inlets to cool the incoming air to whatever extent we could and, somehow, we made it through that day and the very hot afternoon.

We stopped for the night in western New Mexico and found a motel with a "Kitchenette." There were two beds in the room and that wasn't enough for the five children and my parents. A cot had been brought along and my daddy, with a mean look, told me I would sleep on the cot. The three other brothers, including my older brother, would sleep on the bed. My sister, being a toddler, would sleep in the bed with my parents. To me, it was just another case of being singled out for disfavor.

The next day we were in central New Mexico in one of the small towns that are on the route to Albuquerque, I believe it was Gallup. We stopped at a gas station, and we all went to the restrooms as usual, but when I came out, the car and the rest of the family were nowhere to be seen. I thought they must have gone on down the highway and I must try to find them. I ran out onto the shoulder of the road and began running down the road to find them. For whatever reason, I stopped and started walking back to the gas station. There I found the car had been placed on a hydraulic lift and most of the family was in it. That is a bit strange, because why would my daddy and my brothers want to get back in the car when we had been in it for so long, and why would daddy be in it when the mechanical functions of the car were being examined. Had it been me, I would have been under the car with the service people examining the situation firsthand. Years later my mother confirmed that she and my baby sister were in the lady's restroom at the time.

Later that afternoon we arrived in Albuquerque, where my mother's brother, Murray, who was an army career soldier (I think he drove trucks) lived with his wife Wanda. She was of native American Indian heritage and was from southeastern Oklahoma. Their apartment, again, shared a bathroom with the adjoining unit next door (sounds strange to me, but you make do with what you can afford, I guess).

I remember them talking about drinking "Salty Dogs" and being given a mint-flavored, chocolate patty, which I had never tasted before, and I found it to be very nice to eat. "Salty Dogs," I found out later, are a mixture of Vodka, lemon, and grapefruit juice along with a liberal sprinkling of salt, but I think these drinks were made with Gin instead of Vodka.

Don't remember the rest of the way home, but this was the first time I had traveled through Vernon, Oklahoma, which is significant only because that is where you turn off U.S. 287 in Texas and pick up U.S. 70, which routed us back to our home near De Queen, Ar. I would later travel through Vernon as I drove myself and a buddy home from Oregon in my 49 Plymouth coupe, but we didn't travel through Arizona in August on that trip.

Sixth Grade

I no longer had to wear overalls to school, for which I was very thankful, and my teacher was Mrs. Wright. I was thankful for that also because the alternative would have been Mrs. Leslie, who was the school Principal, had a stern reputation and was known for using a school paddle to discipline students, even the girls (that was allowed back then). Mrs. Wright was a kind lady, and I enjoyed being in her class.

At one point some of the boys in the class, being boys that lived inside the city limits of this very small town, decided that they were better than those of us who lived in rural areas outside the city. They started calling me and some others "Country Hicks." Mrs. Wright heard this and soon put a stop to it.

The class was remarkable because the use of the stage and the auditorium was made available for us to attempt to create some stage plays, or other expressive presentations. It was unstructured and I suppose was intended to allow some creativity in our schoolwork. To me, it was also somewhat frustrating, because there being some expectation that I was to create something and had no idea what that was or how to go about it.

One event stands out in my memory and seems to have influenced me because it was so enjoyable. A Magic Show was scheduled for the school, and these were fun, but, being in the sixth grade, we had seen them before and didn't choose to pay the, less than one dollar, admission fee. Those of us who had not paid the fee were instructed to go to Mrs. Leslie's classroom and stay there, unsupervised, for the show's duration. There were several of us boys, mostly all sixth graders, and we started telling stories, and probably jokes, some of those may have been a little lewd. One boy seemed to have a natural gift for storytelling and told several; that passed the time quickly and, for me, made it a very good time well spent.

One rule was enacted that I often ran afoul of; that was that we were to use our recess time to get a drink of water, rather than grabbing a drink as we came back inside after the end of the period. I, and others, wanted to play football during the recess period, and that ended only with the ringing of the bell. Returning inside, naturally I was thirsty and pausing at the water fountain was only a normal urge. Luckily that rule wasn't strictly enforced.

Sidewalk skates were also in use at that time. These had metal wheels, and most were adjustable (with a "key") to fit different foot sizes. One girl wanted me (repeatedly) to try her skates. I did so a few times and developed the ability to skate on the very uneven sidewalk. That girl invited me to a Saturday afternoon party at her home, which was located on the highway coming from town at a place, across from the large city cemetery, called "Browns." I was allowed to attend, and I guess my mother dropped me off there. Later my daddy was to pick me up and I waited for him to do so, but when he failed to come, I started walking home along the edge of the highway. A short while later, my daddy drove up, coming from town, and picked me up; he wasn't happy. He had been waiting in town at a place called Brown's Hatchery, where baby chickens were created and had become increasingly frustrated when I didn't show up.

Summer Before Junior High School

The family took another trip, this time into Oklahoma to, again, visit my father's sister and her family, who lived in Lawton, and friends from Piney Grove Bible Camp who lived in Oklahoma City. The sister's husband, Bill, worked on the nearby Fort Sill Army base and took us on a tour of the base. It was very interesting to me, not only for the military activities and equipment, including some very large helicopters (these had large rotary engines in the front under bulbus cowling that looked like a big nose), some of the artillery shells that seemed huge and other military equipment and some historical sites, including the cell where the Indian war chief Jeronimo had been held. I noted that the baseball fields were perfectly kept, probably by the soldiers there on detail assignment.

Bill also drove us in his car up high on a mountain near the base. Near the summit the engine began to stall, which he said was due to the altitude - although that was only a couple thousand feet above the flat land of the base. I suspect he needed to clean the engine's air filter.

Outside the base and to the northwest was a nature preserve where native buffalo (Bison) roamed amid several lakes. The lakes were very unusual in that they were filled with water weeds that seemed to form a lattice across the entire lake. There was no boating allowed on those lakes, as I remember, and I suspect the weeds would have been a problem for the boat propeller systems, had that been allowed. The family had lunch in a picnic area and at that area, I slightly pushed my younger brother. I had mentioned earlier about the resentment built up because of the whipping I received when he had his bathroom incident. My daddy grabbed me and took me off about one hundred yards away behind some bushes and gave me a whipping with his belt with which he must have hit me about 20 times.

Near Christmas Time, my daddy offered me a chance to earn some "Christmas Money." My weekly allowance was a dime; he offered me $10 to completely plow the garden plot with our garden tractor. I was to use the large "turning plow," which cut a furrow about six inches deep and cast the dirt to the side, effectively "turning over" the soil. One wheel of the tractor ran in the rut of the previous cut and was used as a guide for the next cut. I worked afternoons and Saturdays until I had the garden completely plowed. I was paid the $10 and I judiciously used it for buying Christmas Gifts for the family.

CHAPTER SIX
JUNIOR HIGH
SCHOOL YEARS

Seventh Grade

The Seventh Grade, which was the beginning of Junior High (grades seven, eight, and nine), entailed a switch to the campus which housed the Junior High School and High School. Behind the high school was the football field. The junior high building had previously been the high school. It was a three-story red brick building with a basement, and it seemed rather impressive and regal in its outward appearance. It stood at the west end of De Queen Avenue and was crossed in front by Ninth Street. Those streets were also part of the Hwy 70 route through the town and all that traffic ran past the school and made a turn to the west at the corner of Ninth Street and West Locke Avenue. The whole school complex was located only five city blocks from the county courthouse which sat on its own square block in the center of downtown. One benefit of that was that, if we needed school supplies, we could easily walk downtown during lunch hour. There were no restrictions about staying on campus during those days.

The new city high school sat on an adjacent lot to the south side of the junior high. Other school buildings lay to the south of the new high school and appeared to have been built at the same time.

The football stadium lay to the west of the high school. It may be interesting to note that the stadium had a small concrete pillar monument indicating that the field had been constructed by the WPA government program. That could have been in 1939, as I believe the monument indicated. One additional fact about the stadium was that it had only two single-stall restrooms, one for the men and one for the ladies. In the men's (I don't know about the ladies) the walls were covered in witty sayings, poems and whatever. One could get an education by visiting that stall. In all the years I was there, there was never any effort to cover up those inscriptions.

In the seventh grade, we (the boys) were introduced to higher education with hazing by the older male students in the school with a ritual called "Bumping." This involved the new seventh graders being grabbed by a group of older boys who would then spread the legs of the victim and swing him into a tree where he would be struck in the groin area by the tree. Luckily, I was struck by the tree in an area on the buttocks, rather than the genital area. No harm was done to me, and I don't know of anyone who suffered any damage or temporary pain by having this done to them. This was the last year for that tradition.

P.E., Physical Education, was introduced in the seventh grade, and it was an uncomfortable experience. We had to "dress out" in shorts and a tee shirt and that meant changing out of our regular clothes in a locker room. Our dressing room was in the basement room below the basketball court/auditorium of the main high school and was not the best of facilities. We had a wire basket in a rack of baskets to store our clothes while in the class and our workout clothes when we weren't. It was secured with a combination lock. I suppose there was a shower there, but I don't remember it, and we were usually hard pressed to change our clothes and get to the next class anyway. My next class that year was a science class held in the basement of the school, which, luckily, was cooler than the classrooms in the upper stories. The teacher, Mrs. Morris, noted our red-faced and hot states, and tried to help as much as possible.

One experience does stand out in my memory and that was seeing an older boy dressing, he had no underwear under his jeans. Jeans at that time did not have a zippered fly, but rather, had buttons, usually metal buttons, and I strongly remember him buttoning up the front of his jeans and thinking that he must live in a very poor family.

That year there was some kind of health program exam involving the county government, and possibly the state government that was conducted at the school. All the boys and girls were separated and given an examination. I don't remember much about this, but the girls were given some kind of upper body covering, like a paper drape, to wear during the exams. This was never done again at the schools that I am aware of.

Small "Blimps"

This happened during the summer when I turned 12 years old. On a mid-afternoon on a sunny day, I walked out into the field in front of our house and proceeded in a southwesterly direction. I don't remember my objective for doing this; there was a creek at the bottom of the hill that flowed from the adjacent land and that may have had something to do with my mission. As I walked past the crest of the hill, I looked off in a southeasterly direction where, above the large pine treetops on an adjoining section of land south of our newly acquired 10-acre field, I saw three large round silvery spheres floating in the sky about 100 feet above the treetops. These were about 10 – 15 feet in diameter and floated freely in the air with some up-and-down motion as I perceived them.

My immediate thought was "Humm, those must be small blimps." I looked away in the direction I was originally headed, and never looked back. Had I known what I know now, I would have frozen in place and watched them until they disappeared. Years later, I saw, on television, a film taken by a Navy photographer that showed what I perceived as a similar craft moving at high speed, without any evidence of a propulsion system, through the air near the field.

Many years later, I had dinner with a man who related that, in his military service, he had been recruited into, and had served, in the NSA (National Security Agency). We discussed a lot of things, and I related my experience with the "small Blimps."

Nothing was said but I was left with the strong impression that the small crafts I saw were not blimps at all. My personal belief, after gathering much information through the years from whatever sources I could find, is that these were extraterrestrial craft: UFOs, if you will, but not "flying saucers.

Many, many, years I told my story to a gathering of my brothers and daddy. His reaction was like, although nothing was stated: "That's an amazing story and you could be right about what they were. It's amazing that happened here."

The Calf Program

To upgrade our cattle herd, we had about seven cows, my daddy initiated a program that introduced registered Polled Herford bloodlines into mix. Mostly we had dairy cows, but bred them to beef producing bulls, producing a cross-bred group of cows. A polled Herford heifer was selected from a herd on a farm near Broken Bow, Oklahoma and brought to our farm. This became designated as my older brother's breeding cow, and the first calf was to become my cow. The first calf of my cow was to become my younger brother's cow, etc. All future offspring, after the first, would remain the property of the producing cow's designated owner. I think that the partial objective of all of this was to provide some funds for special things when the calves were sold.

Unfortunately, purebred breeding didn't continue and the first calf that remained as mine was a beefy-looking animal with "brindle" hair (striped with alternating back and reddish-brown streaks), not a Polled Herford. The second was a tall, rangy, and somewhat thin animal with hair that turned from red to black where it was not white: not a beef cow. A third cow was a more Jersey-looking animal, also not a beef cow.

My luck with these cows turned out to be not very good. The first cow, while pastured on the land north of our farm, along with more of the herd, got her foot caught in some net-wire fencing left partially buried in the ground. She was unable to free herself and we found her dead later. The second cow was due to have a calf and at the time she was due, my daddy initiated a search with me and my older brother also searching for the calf, none was found. Eventually, my daddy more closely examined the cow and saw that the tail of the unborn calf was sticking out of the mother cow.

The calf was supposed to have the head come out first in a normal birth. My daddy tried pulling on the calf's tail until it broke away from its body. Further efforts were abandoned. The cow was moved closer to the house and placed in the calf pasture near the barn and left to die, which she did in about a week.

When my daddy was attempting to pull the calf, I was watching nearby and he turned to me and said: "I fear for you, God's going to strike you down!" I was about 14 years old at the time. My opinion was that, when in the years following, that didn't happen, he was disappointed.

The third cow later developed an intestinal infection and died. With my mother's help and direction, we made a wood pile, pulled the cow on top of it and burned it. The cow was consumed by the fire and nothing, but ashes remained. With that, I was out of the cow program. Was that because of God's wrath?

Harvesting Beef

Somewhere along in my early teenage years, a chest freezer was procured for storage of meat and other foods for the family. It was placed in a corner of the dining room just inside the door leading from the living room and cleared that door by only a few inches. My younger siblings had a tricycle they rode in the house and, to protect the corner of the new freezer from the scratches that could be caused by the tricycle, daddy built a guard of wood slats to cover the corner. It worked very well, as I recall. The brand of the freezer was "Unico" and was bought through the local Farmer's Cooperative store. It worked very well for our purposes.

To utilize the new freezer, a male beef yearling was harvested. On the selected morning in the cool/cold temperatures, the animal was led to a place by an oak tree outside of the chicken laying house. The animal seemed, to me, to have sensed that whatever was in store for him wasn't good, as he stood still with his head lowered and tied to a rope. One shot from a .22 rifle in the center of his forehead hit him and he immediately fell to the ground. The slaughtering process soon began.

A wagon singletree was again used to attach the animal's rear legs to a rope block and tackle hoist. The hoist was stung to a sturdy branch oak tree above the area. The animal was hoisted, and the process began. My older brother and I were soon involved in skinning the animal and removing the intestines from the area. The thick skin had to be separated from the underlying tissues by using a knife and cutting along the boundary between the skin and the flesh while pulling on the skin. It took some time to do this of course, as this was a very large animal. My daddy handled the separation of the animal's genitalia and had his penis in his hand as he said to us: "This is his tally whacker."

The animal was gutted and, again, a washtub was used to collect all of that as it fell from the slit in the animal's belly. These were, again, deposited in the forest for scavengers.

Once all of these processes had been completed, the carcass was wrapped in a sheet, placed in the bed of the pickup, and driven to a butchering and freezing facility in De Queen. Future beefs had to be delivered live to the processing facility, which was okay with me.

Grace Baptist Church

Three families that had been attending church services at the Piney Grove Bible Camp, one family from the Union Community Church north of the town and a fifth family from inside the town, united to form a new church to be located within the city limits of De Queen. Only a vacant lot existed where the church was to be built. That lot was on the westernmost north-south most heavily used street in the town, Ninth Street, which tied to roads leading north and west into rural areas surrounding the city.

The church was built with a Loan from The Horatio National Bank, rather than a loan from the bank in De Queen. Horatio, Arkansas is a smaller town located about 10 miles south of De Queen. The significance of all of that is/was unclear, except to say that the Horatio Bank may have been willing to take a larger risk than the De Queen bank; after all, the group requesting the loan were tenuously associated, were not wealthy families and the organization was not fully assured to last, at least in my opinion.

Initially, the church group held their services in the rented American Legion Hall, in town. That worked well except for the times when the legion pre-empted the hall without notice. "Bob and Pearl" from the Dallas Theological Seminary made weekly trips to De Queen to serve as the ministers to the church. Pearl was a very talented musician and played piano regularly and the marimba at special times. I remember talking with Bob about his car: a Dodge with a "Red Ram" V8, which he said, made the trips go more quickly.

The church was built with some hired labor, such as framing and brickwork, but a large part of it was done with labor supplied by the members and their families. My brother and I worked there a lot and mixed a lot of concrete to pour the floors. At one point, while other work was being done, I picked up a broom and began sweeping areas of the previously poured and finished flooring. One of the men commented "A lot of good work is being done by that boy with the broom." The floors certainly looked better after being cleared of the mortar droppings and other debris on them, and they certainly wanted me to continue. I wasn't so sure I wanted to do that, but I did.

The new pastor and his wife "Art and Shirley" arrived as missionaries after the church became affiliated with The General Baptist Convention, headquartered, I believe, in Rapid City Iowa. Art was the owner of a factory in Massachusetts and was independently wealthy. Certainly, this assignment was new for them and for us as members. Art and Shirley purchased a lot across the street from the church and had a frame house built there, it had a great new feature, it had a large air conditioning unit installed in a window in the living room. Just before they moved in, I was, somehow, designated to clean all the windows, inside and out with a pink window clearing liquid that dried to a chalky substance that was then wiped away. I did that as I had been told and I think I did a good job. No pay was associated with this task.

Other work in building the church involved using an over-the-table power saw that could be set to cut angles for the trim pieces. I became proficient at using that saw; I was probably thirteen at the time. Other tasks I performed included using a hand-held "star" drill with a hammer to make holes in the concrete for attaching bolts that were necessary for securing the interior walls to the floor. After a bit of instruction, I completed all the holes that were needed at that time and afterward completed more.

Later the wooden pews arrived, built by a church member who had a woodworking factory in the city. It was selected to color them with a lightly applied whitish liquid stain applied with a compressed air spray gun. Pastor "Art" was working at doing the application, then he handed the spray gun to me and said "proceed." I started spraying with a back-and-forth motion from about a foot away from the surface of the pews. The stain settled on the pews nicely and Pastor Art commented: "He's doing a better job than I did, and he's never done this before in his life."

This being a Baptist Church, it was deemed necessary to have a baptistery built into the church structure. This was accommodated by forming a concrete pit in the front of the auditorium that was under a removeable floor that later became the choir loft (of sorts). The pit was dark and unlined with any tile, it was indeed a foreboding place that, in my opinion, would cause any convert to have second thoughts about being baptized there.

Instead of using the pit, when the parents of us teenagers and younger children decided that we would be baptized, a spot in the Rolling Fork River, which ran through a church member's property, was chosen. We weren't asked if we would choose to be baptized, or did we have any religious conviction that would make this meaningful to us. It was just: you will do this! On the appointed day, a Saturday, or Sunday afternoon, the families gathered on the bank of the river for the ceremonies to begin.

Provisions had been made for changing our clothes after the dunking, by using farm equipment to cut down the tall weeds in a way that created a circular changing area at the end of a short lane through the weeds, one for the boys and one for the girls. The tall weeds afforded all the privacy that was necessary, but, of course, the stobs left in the ground at the weeds' base were a hazard if you stepped on one.

One by one, we were summoned out into the water and ceremoniously dipped backward into the water. Because it was not of my choosing, I felt no significance in the event, other than being embarrassed and glad no one besides the church members were present.

Junior High Sports

In the seventh grade it did not enter my mind to try to play on the junior high "Cubs" football team, even though I had really enjoyed football in elementary school. I did want to play basketball and my older brother, and I both attended the "tryouts" for the team. Luckily, I was chosen for the team on the "third string," which included some other boys in my class. I didn't know it at the time, but our group was a "developmental" group for coming years. The coach was the same one who coached the football team, Coach Williams. We "dressed out" (we wore team uniforms) and were on the bench only at home games. My older brother was a ninth grader and was on the team as well in the "varsity" group.

The uniforms we were given to wear were white (the varsity colors were black and gold) and the pants were intended to be worn as hip huggers. I didn't know that and pulled the pants up to my normal beltline, this exposed my hip bones under the shorts. The coach started to say something to me to get me to lower the pants, but never finished what he was about to say, I continued to wear the pants that way, but I was very uncomfortable as I did so. I don't remember playing in any game, but it was good to be on the team.

In the eighth grade I decided that I wanted to play football and at the end of the summer, in August, went to team practices. There wasn't enough team equipment "suits," which included the pads and helmet, to equip all those who wanted to "try out" for the team. I didn't get a suit, but instead wore shorts and a tee shirt and, after the calisthenics, watched the scrimmage action while on one knee behind the offensive group. Attrition took place among those trying out and eventually, I got a "suit."

Later during the fall, I got to play in a scrimmage, and I still remember that first play; I was playing on the offensive line at the "end" position and was supposed to block someone in the defensive linebacker position. I went to do that (and probably missed), then someone came up behind me and threw an elbow into my back. It was as if to say, "Welcome to football!"

Prior to the start of the summer practice, the players (and prospective players) had to undergo a physical exam. When I came up, the hydrocele was detected by the doctor, who summoned the coach over and said to him, "This boy will need protection." It was decided that the jockey strap would be sufficient, and I was to be allowed to play. The boy standing behind me and heard the conversation, and being a typical young teenager, didn't understand what he heard and once, later, accused me later of being "ruptured." That's all that ever came from this event.

I also had a problem that I didn't tell anyone about. Earlier in the summer, on a Sunday afternoon, my older brother and I, and another teen from a family at the church, went to the woodworking shop run by that family. A young colt was being kept there and, despite being told not to, we decided to try to ride that colt. When it came my time to ride, after mounting up and starting off across the pasture, the colt began bucking and I was thrown off. As luck would have it, I landed on the ground astraddle a crawfish mound. It was in exactly the right position to keep me from rolling to one side, or the other, and I took the shock directly in my spine.

Crawfish (we called them "crawdads") live, outside of standing water and streams, on low lying land that isn't more than a few feet above the underground water table. They build mounds, (some call them "chimneys") with a hole down the middle, of mud balls up to about 10 inches in height and 4, or 5 inches in diameter at the base. They dig down into the earth to the water table and, apparently, live a lot of the time in that water. If the water table drops, they can always dig deeper.

As a result of the fall (and especially the landing) I felt a sharp pain in the middle upper region of my spine. I could hardly breathe for three weeks afterward and was feeling pain with every breath. But I told no one about this because we weren't supposed to be riding the horse. I found out, years later, that mine was the same type of injury that pilots who eject out of airplanes often sustain when the rocket motor fires and accelerates them out of the plane.

During some of the early football practices, I was occasionally bothered by that spinal pain, but I persisted, and the pain eventually subsided.

During one of the mid-season practices, one of the boys playing at a halfback position got the ball and was running into the line of scrimmage on the right side. As he ran into the line of scrimmage, he was hit on the legs by an opposing player trying to make a tackle. When the hit occurred, I heard a loud "crack" noise that was highly unusual. The player got up and reported that his knee was hurt. The coach told him to go to another area and try to loosen it up by jogging. The player did that but was unable to ease the pain. Turns out the player had a cracked kneecap that left him walking with a limp. He never played sports again.

Later, near the end of the season after we had played our last scheduled game, The ninth graders went on to practice with the high school team, which still had games on their schedule. That left us eight graders as the "varsity" team, as it were. We weren't familiar with that term and merely considered ourselves to be "First Stringers." I moved myself into the position of being the starting right end and that became the position I played the next year.

This new team played a nighttime practice game against the team from the town of Foreman, which is south of De Queen and Horatio, across Little River and about 15 miles from there into the next county. In that game a Foreman player, who had been a student in my school and a friend, played against each other, but we greeted each other on the field after the game. Our meeting was observed by the coach, who asked me about what was going on. I told him the player was a friend, but I didn't treat him like it during the game. The coach was satisfied with that, and nothing further was said.

Another scrimmage game was played later as a night game, this was with Texas Junior High School players in Texarkana. It was played on a practice field that was completely stripped of grass and it was only mud after recent rains. We, nonetheless, played that game under the lights and slogged through the black mud. It was a very one-sided affair and in the Texas team's favor, so much so that the referees started calling our punts, after they had landed on the ground untouched, our ball, when I covered it, or as in the last case, only touched it on the ground. My coach, however, admonished me later to cover it with my body on the ground. That would have meant falling onto, and into, the mud and in this case, that, in my view, wasn't necessarily required.

Junior High Basketball

Basketball tryouts after football ended and I went to the tryouts without any idea, after the football experience, that I would make the team. As the tryouts proceeded, I wasn't given much playing time and thought my chances were very slim. I asked the coach if he had his team and, apparently, he didn't like that, and I wasn't chosen. I didn't realize that having been a development player the previous year, I had a good chance of making the team. With my state of mind at that point, it may have been a good thing to not play that year.

At home, in addition to basketball hoop that had been attached to the smoke house, my brother and I erected a basketball goal and backboard in a pasture area just outside the garden. We cut a medium sized tree for a pole, trimmed off all branches, built a backboard, and attached the goal. We erected the pole in the pasture by digging a hole with the posthole diggers and planting the goal assembly in the hole. It was a good and usable goal and the ground in front of it became our court. Eventually, the grass on the court was worn away, leaving a smooth surface to bounce the ball on. The first basketball we had was a ball with a leather lace up seam that was given to my older brother as a Christmas present. We played a lot of basketball with it.

We played a lot of one-on-one games and one time I played against my brother and another player his age in a one-on-two situation. That must have helped my skills and confidence, as the next year I was back on the basketball team.

Eighth Grade School Year

The new school year brought with some significant changes; A new Junior High building had been erected on land between the previous old building Junior High and the high school. A new gymnasium stood where the old school building had been. The new junior high building had been built with open hallways to the outside, meaning that there was no protection from the cold during the winter and we had to wear coats when changing classrooms. Also, there was no protection from the rain, except for the building overhang over the walkways. The concrete surface of the walking areas was smoothly finished, which was great, except for the times when the surfaces were coated with condensed water from the humidity, those surfaces then became very slippery. A new cafeteria was located at the west end near the football stadium.

It was necessary for two students to share lockers, which were located on the interior walkways connecting the two outsides. This led to an incident where my locker partner wrote the word "F***" in large letters on the first sheet of my clipboard. I found it, took off the page, folded it and put it in my pocket. Evidently, I failed to remove that page from my pocket before my jeans were laundered. My mother apparently found it and must have given it to Daddy, because, when I was riding alone with him in the pickup, he spoke to me about that and said

"That's something you can just forget about. "That was the sum of any and all advice I got from him about sex education.

Back at the school, it was notable to me that the previous tradition of "Bumping" of the incoming seventh graders somehow got lost. Apparently, no one really noticed, or cared, about the change as far as I knew.

On TV during that year (1958), "The Mickey Mouse Show" became popular and was a favorite of many of the boys that I knew. Some of them wanted to form a fan club for "Mouseketeer" Annette Funicello, who was certainly a pretty, talented, and well-developed young lady. I think a letter to her was written and, surprisingly, a reply was received.

In the spring of that year, one day I suddenly began thinking about a girl named Janice, who had been in my Fifth-Grade class, but had since disappeared. The next day Janice walked up to the school to visit. I've always thought this was more than a coincidence. I don't know if we ever met during that visit, but something foretold me of it.

That year the school athletics coach taught my math class. A part of that class was working with fractions. I passed the class, but somehow didn't learn to solve fractions. The next year, in Algebra class, I taught myself how to work with fractions.

In English class, some of the assignments were giving book reports, where we would read the book then stand up at the front of the class and deliver our report. I must have done well, because at the end of the year, I was one of several who were exempted from the final test.

Peach Packing Shed

During the summer, prior to my ninth grade, my older brother and I got a chance to work in a peach harvesting operation in the neighboring town of Horatio. We were given jobs in the packing shed where harvested peaches were brought for sorting and placement in bushel baskets. Afterward those baskets would be loaded onto trucks and hauled north (I think the destination for some of them was Kansas City). Horatio peaches were known to be delicious, especially the big, rosy-skinned Elbertas and there were many orchards in the area.

My brother and I worked principally on the end of the packing line where the baskets would arrive on a conveyor upside down. They had to then be turned upright with a special device I call an "inverter," before having the basket lids installed. Our pay was $0.50 per hour, but that was good money for us, and we were glad to get it. My job at the end was to run the basket inverter, where I would ram the upside-down baskets across the rollers at the end of the conveyor belt and into the machine, then I would operate the machine by rapidly pulling a lever through a 180-degree arc, thusly turning the basket, with the peaches inside, upright. The basket was then pushed out the other side onto rollers where other workers would attach the basket lids.

Most of the other workers in the shed were local teenagers, and, of course, some friendships were formed, and I got to know several who I would later play against in basketball games and attend college with.

At the end of the season, one of the pretty young girls my age invited me to a party at her home. The trouble was that my older brother had not been invited and wasn't going to drive me there, so I had no way to go there. I subsequently got an angry letter saying that she had been the only one there without a date. I wrote back to her, but never received a reply.

One notable event occurred during the summer is that I found out about, after school started, that one of the "Jerry's" in my class (there were three) had been killed in a motorcycle accident. At another time, another youth was reported to have lost a leg in a motorcycle collision with a train; you wonder how that could happen.

Typhoid

During the summer, my mother was diagnosed with Typhoid, which was thought to have come from the well water we were using as the family drinking source. That was never proven as far as I know. As a result, the family was visited by a health nurse from the county government, and we were instructed to change the family's toilet arrangements. As a result, a six-foot-deep pit was dug, lined with concrete and an outhouse built on top of it. The capacity inside the house was made to be a "two-holer," where two people could use the facility at once, if needed. The paper supply was always the old Sears and Roebucks and Montgomery Wards catalogues, which worked okay until only the glossy colored pages remained.

The family was also required to receive once-a-week typhoid shots for three weeks. The family took the series of shots on Saturdays and each shot left us very ill for a few hours afterwards. We had to lie down during that period to recuperate.

On the day of the last shot, my mother told me I could lay on the bed with her, which I did, but I was somewhat puzzled by her request.

The New Well

As a further consequence of typhoid in the home, it was decreed by Daddy that a new well would be dug to supply the family with uncontaminated (possibly) water. A dowser was summoned and a site in the front yard was designated as the spot for the well. It was further decreed that my older brother and I would dig the well.

After learning about the dowser's methods, I began to experiment with dowsing. I learned to take a forked stick, preferably one cut from a branch of a green (live) tree, hold it inverted with my two hands on the ends of the fork and walk around waiting for the stick to dip. When underground water was present, the stick would start to dip on its own down toward the ground. I learned that the attraction of the stick to the water could be very powerful, even to the point where the ends of the fork held in my hands would twist as I tried to hold back the tip of the fork. Dowsers were/are also called "Water Witches," and I seem to be one.

At the chosen site for the new well, my daddy erected a hoisting structure he called a "horse." It had A-Frames on each end supporting a strong thick crosspiece to which a pulley and rope were attached in the center of it. On one end he constructed a windlass for winding the rope that would connect to the five-gallon bucket. That bucket would be used to raise the dugout dirt, and to raise and lower the digger into and out of the well. A safety device on the side of the windlass was devised using a plywood disc with notches cut into the outer edge with a wood slat "brake" that would engage the wheel and stop it if it tried to turn backwards during a bucket haul-out. That was an ingenious device and a welcomed safety measure, but there was one major flaw: it did not work when lowering the bucket into the well, and lowering the bucket with the digger inside was the only way to get down in the well for more digging. That had to be done without the safety brake.

As luck would have it, at about the 30-foot level, as I was lowering my older brother into the well, the handle of the windlass slipped out of my hand, then it flew around in an arc and struck me on the top of my head almost knocking me unconscious. My brother, inside the lowering bucket fell to the bottom of the well. I don't know how far his fall was, but I would estimate it was about 10 feet. Luckily, he wasn't hurt, as I remember. After the fall, rather than putting my brother at risk, I volunteered to do the digging from then on. He says I dug the last ten feet by myself.

At the end of the 44 feet of digging, we still had not struck water. The well was a narrow hole about two and a half to three feet wide, down to about forty feet below the surface. I found out later that the earth in that area was not very stable and a cave-in possibility was not remote.

The dowser was again summoned to verify his findings. He is reported to have said the water channel was seven feet away from the well and we had missed it.

Despite not finding water, I had developed a huge boil on the back of my right hand during the process. It was then deemed that the well would be developed to completion as if it were a good new water well. Daddy devised a removable wood slat form that he (as I found out much later) and a neighbor used to pour a concrete lining for the well. He also procured and installed an electric water-pump and pressure holding tank for the well. He even built a double-walled pump house that had sawdust between the sides of the walls to provide insulation against freezing temperatures. Then he ran a gutter from the roof of the house to the well to collect rainwater. That all failed to provide the new water supply that was needed and the water that came off the roof was stained a dark brown from the effects of the oak tree overhanging the house.

The Drilled Well

In the Spring of the year following the disaster with our newly dug well, the drilling of a deep subterranean well was arranged with a drilling company. A spot was chosen in the back yard, the drilling rig was moved in, and the drilling began. The rig was an odd-looking contraption with a Model A Ford, four-cylinder engine. A visitor to the rig stopped and listened to the smooth sounds of that engine and said he could tell that engine was running exceptionally well. The function of the rig was to repeatedly raise and then drop a very long steel cylinder (about 12 feet long), which had cutting surfaces on the sides and bottom. This enabled the bits to cut into the rock in multiple places as it dropped.

Occasionally, a long tube that filled from the bottom, was dropped into the hole to draw out the mud at the bottom that had been created by the drill and the ground water. That "mud" was deposited a short distance away from the hole and, surprisingly, a lot of it was yellow in color. Periodically the workers would use a mirror to direct sunlight into the hole to see near the bottom.

The drilling progressed until the water-containing strata was struck at a depth below 200 feet. That water was in a stratum of very fine white sand, and, sometimes, had a smell of oil to it.

A well casing of thin galvanized steel sections was assembled and placed in the well. A day, or a few days afterward, the earth shifted and collapsed the walls of the casing. The only way to fix that was to start over and drill a new well. The rig was moved over a couple of feet and the drilling began again. This time the well was lined with oil well casing that solved the earth shifting issues.

It was interesting to me to see the drillers secure electrical power to their welding system by removing the power meter from its house connection, then connecting their equipment directly to the incoming power line connections. This provided them with free electricity of sufficient power to complete their job. Afterwards, the meter was reinstalled. Power companies have since started putting seals on their meters to prevent this from happening.

The insertion of the pump was a new and different challenge; the pump chosen, rather than being a submersible set in the bottom of the well, was a "Jet" pump with the motor on top of the well. For the jet to work it had to be lowered into the water to a sufficient depth to be well below the water level. Two large plastic pipes, with the jet on the bottom, had to be lowered into the depths of the well.

To assist in lowering the pipes into the well, my daddy had attached a wire wrapped around a spindle so that he could unwind it as the pipes were lowered. This was all well and good, but the weight of the pipes was increasing as the pipes were lowered. I was helping to manage the pipes above the well and keep them moving across the grass. At one point Daddy was struggling with the weight of it. It was all he could do to keep them from dropping into the well. If that had happened, then the whole project to be ruined. Somehow the pipes were successfully lowered, and the pump attached. The new well was then ready to supply water to the family, which it did from then on.

It is interesting to me to note that I was helping him do a lot of things when my older brother wasn't. One of those was when an oak tree near a chicken house was cut down and sawed into blocks for splitting into firewood. We were using a two-man crosscut saw with Daddy on one end and, either me or my older brother, on the other end. At one point Daddy told me to replace him and that I seemed to have a better sense of rhythm in drawing the saw back and forth. I was helping him, but he was still, otherwise, showing no approval.

When I was thirteen, I had moved a sack of cow feed into the feed storage area; he was there and, out of the blue, said to me: "Quit your bitching." It was like a line he had rehearsed and was looking for an opportunity to use it.

Ninth Grade Football

The school year began with football practice in late August. During the first days it was always hot, and we had "Two-a-Days" practice schedules, which meant we would start the first practice at about 9:00 in the morning, end about 11:00, then come back about 4:00 in the afternoon for a second session. During those first days, it was common for boys to get sick to their stomachs and some would "Feed the grasshoppers," meaning they would vomit on the ground. I did that in the ninth grade, but not in later years. During those days, it wasn't allowed for us to drink water during the practices. I learned, eventually in later years, to catch sweat coming off my face in the chinstrap of my helmet and would then suck on that to relieve my mouth dryness.

I survived the first practice then went home and, after consuming a lot of fluids, laid down to rest. At the next practice, in the afternoon, I found it easier to tolerate the heat and the physical demands as, apparently, the conditioning had begun to take hold.

One of the exercises we did that year was designed to strengthen our necks. We would work in pairs; one player would be on his hands and knees and the other player would sit astride his back, while pushing down on the player's helmet. The player on the ground would push against the resistance and move his head from side to side. The players would then switch positions and repeat the exercise.

I was the starting right end on offense, as I had been when the season ended last year. There weren't many passes thrown in the games that year and I remember there was only one passing route-pattern that we had to run. It was a crossing route where the two ends ran out into the defensive backfield, then both cut toward the center at 45-degree angles. This was supposed to confuse the coverage and give the quarterback optional targets. We ran that play in a game with Mena, at their field. As the other End and, as I neared the crossing point, the ball was thrown but too far in front of me to catch. I assumed it was meant for the other player and I pulled back my outstretched hands. The ball then sailed to the other player and hit him on his thigh, falling incomplete. I don't think any more passes were thrown that season.

Our last game of the season was with Texarkana Junior High and their team was designated as "The Piggies," since the high school team was known as The Hogs" after the Razorback Hogs of the University of Arkansas. I don't remember much about that game, except that my uniform was unusually clean after the game. That could have been because the field had a good covering of grass, unlike our home field, which served as both the practice field and game field for both the junior and senior school teams.

When we arrived, later that night, back at our school, my daddy was waiting there in the darkness in his pickup to take me home. We took our gear down to the locker room, then the bus was going to take us to "Hills" restaurant for an after-game meal This was the normal procedure for out-of-town football games. My daddy wanted me to skip the meal and come home with him, but I was hungry and really wanted something to eat. Daddy finally agreed to that and allowed me to board the bus, which took us to "Hills" restaurant where I was served a real "chicken-fried "steak, along with the mashed potatoes and gravy sides. I loved it. My mother had served fried steak before, but it was nothing like this.

Daddy had closed the door to the pickup and sat there until the bus brought me back to the school. He could have driven on down to the restaurant and had something to eat himself (and probably visited with other parents and coaches) then we could have left for home earlier than we did, but that was not him…

Basketball Season

In the middle of the season, on a Wednesday night, I was preparing to go to an out-of-town game; when my daddy learned of it, he immediately said "No, you have to go to Prayer Meeting!" So, I didn't go to the game and the coach was understandably upset, and I just explained it off as a transportation issue. Afterwards he made sure I had a ride, at least, near my home (he dropped me off at the highway and I walked the rest of the way).

At the last of the season, there was a "County Championship Tournament" in the nearby city of Lockesburg; their team was known as the "Blue Darters." The final game was played between the blue Darters and my team "The De Queen Leopard Cubs." The game was tight and, right at the end, the coach sent me out to play. Somehow, I was fouled and given a "Free Throw." It was a "one-and one" situation, where if you make the first one, you get to try a second. I made both shots and the game continued. Again, I was fouled and sent to the free throw line. Again, it was a "one and one" opportunity and, as luck would have it, I, again, made both shots. This was enough for my team to win the game and claim the championship.

In the locker room afterwards, another player came up to me and happily said "If you were a girl, I'd kiss you!" Well, I wasn't, and he didn't, and thankfully so, but at a class reunion in recent years, he recounted the game events and told me he was sure that I was going to miss those shots; but that I hadn't missed them (and he was, apparently, greatly relieved). I asked him if he remembered what he said in the dressing room and he said he did not. I told him then and we had a big laugh about it all.

The Christmas Party

The teenage group at the church planned a Christmas Party, attendance at which was virtually mandatory, and I and my older brother attended. One of the girls from another family and I were feeling some mutual attraction and agreed that although I wasn't allowed to date until I was 16 by Daddys out-of-the-blue decree made previously (he had put no similar restriction on my older brother), we would spend some time together at the party. She and I reasoned that, since we both would be attending the party anyway, technically, it wasn't a date.

My older brother, however, had different ideas, after observing the girl and me at the party. When he and I got home my older brother immediately ran up to Daddy and told him: "Jerry had a date!" I said nothing and Daddy looked at me with a look I always remember; it was like "Ah ha! I've got you now!" He said and did nothing to punish me, however, as I was fully expecting.

The tattletale report by my older brother was nothing new; he had a pattern of taking every opportunity he had to get me into trouble and for every little thing he thought was the slightest bit out of line he would say "I'm going to tell daddy!" I don't know how much he did that, but his relationship with Daddy was certainly much different from mine.

The pattern of one brother being in a good relationship with Daddy, while another was despised was, as I understand, pretty much repeated with my two younger brothers, with the older being in his favor and the younger one not.

Cutting Wood

For some time that winter, my older brother and I had been cutting down Red Oak trees in the woods of Mr. Turner's property to replenish the heating wood supply in our home. We would take the two-man crosscut saw, make the needed notch in one side of the base of the tree, then saw through it from the other side until the tree would fall. We would then trim the limbs off the trunk with an axe, then saw the tree trunk, which was laying on the ground, into approximately 18-inch sections.

We would then stand the sections on one end and split them into multiple sticks that would be suitable for placing in the wood stove in our home later. We did this by using the family's single double-bladed "chopping axe." We kept it sharp with a file and it worked well. To split a log, it helped to first look at the center of the log closely. In doing so, I could see small pre-existing cracks radiating out of the center core. Striking the log with the blade of the axe aligned with those cracks would, most easily, split the log. That, of course, required some skill and practice in swinging the axe and having it strike exactly where it was cracked. If I was lucky, I could split the log with one swing of the axe. Somehow, I remember my grandmother Zona working with me there and she had noticed and was impressed (at least she gave me that impression from her body motions) that I had split a log with one strike of the axe.

My brother and I worked in the cold and the snow, cutting and splitting a batch of wood and loading it into the pickup. Daddy took it and sold it to a fellow church member for $4.00. I think he gave us the money, but I was thoroughly amazed and disappointed that he had sold it for so little, after all our hard work.

Hauling Gravel

At other times, during the Spring of that year, my older brother and I were sent on Saturday mornings to a local county-owned gravel pit. These are places where naturally formed collections of small rocks are in the earth at the surface, and lower. These areas could be mined for use in making the roads useable in all weather. We shoveled the rocky mixture, usually mixed with sand, into the bed of the pickup, then hauled it home. There we would shovel it out onto the circle driveway that ran up the hill and under the trees, usually on the upward slope of the entry side. We would usually make two such trips on a single

Saturday, which would take about six hours to complete. We did this many times and I remember Elvis Presley's hit "All Shook Up" playing on the radio at that time.

Incidents at School

During early January, five of us on the basketball team were alone in a classroom for what should have been a Study Hall period, albeit unsupervised. We were sitting at desks arranged in rows, one behind the other. Some of the boys decided, as a prank, to turn around to then scatter the person's behind them books and everything else on the floor. The other players hadn't reacted badly to this, and I thought I should participate, so I turned around and scattered the books behind me off the desk. The player behind me reacted badly and attacked me ferociously, so much so that all I remember was being thrown against the cinder block wall located across the room from where we were and striking the back of my head against the wall. After feeling my head strike the wall, I started to lose consciousness and felt myself sagging toward the floor. I'm sure I had a concussion, but I went home, and no medical assistance was sought. The next day I had an Algebra first semester exam, and I did badly, but I passed the course.

I reported this to the coach and both of us got two licks with a large heavy school paddle. All the players that had been in the room were told to by the coach to "settle this among ourselves." I apologized, but the other players never did, and the one even threatened to "Get on you again," but that never happened, or was ever attempted. Later, in our high school years we got along well.

At another time, this in the Spring of my eighth-grade year, during a lunch period, several of us boys were sitting on the steps leading to the rear entrance of the gymnasium. For whatever reason, the boys began comparing the hair on their legs (boys will be boys). This led to one of the boys, who was bigger and more bearish than I was, deciding to scuffle with me. This evolved into a fist fight, but I never got hit. I had been reading some material and stories about boxing and decided to use what I knew. I popped him in the face with a "One-Two" left-right combination and that took all the fight out of him. I remembered that, during a boxing match, one needs to keep moving, so I began circling him. He just stood there not moving as I did this, eventually I decided the fight was over and walked away from the scene.

A lot of other students at the school had gathered at the scene to watch the fight. As I was walking away, I walked past a girl who said I was a "quitter' for walking away. I just let it pass, she could think whatever she wanted, and I would have nothing to do with her.

Later that afternoon, the other boy and I were in a group undergoing football spring training (of a sort) during the last school period of the day. He had developed a severe black eye, and the coach noticed it. He stopped to examine it and asked how he got that? One of the other players, said "*********** must have hit him." The coach came by and gave me an open-handed swat on the rear but said nothing. I don't know if that was disapproval, or approval, for what had happened. Nothing further came of this incident, but I was not ever again bothered by that individual.

The Girlfriend

During the Ninth Grade a relationship evolved in a very natural manner between myself and a pretty girl in my class who had hair that was so blond it was almost white. During the lunch hour we would find ourselves in the dark hallway next to the school cafeteria. It wasn't that the hallway was dark, it was just that the light could only come from the open ends of it. There we leaned against the wall and talked almost every day.

This was, of course, noticed by other class members and before the end of the year those classmates were saying, "I sure you will do well in the sawmill business," because her father was in that business. But this was all not to be. When I returned at the beginning of the next year, she was gone. Apparently, her family had moved from the town, and I had no idea where that was. That was, I guess, one of the attributes of operating a sawmill: it had to be moved where the forests were being harvested. We lived only about three miles apart, but we had no telephone and the only social interaction I had during the summer was with the church group.

I found out years later that she had written me many letters that never made it to me. My mother found her in a nursing home dying from a brain tumor. She told my mother about us and her efforts. If I had gotten her letters, it may not have made any difference, as time and space issues were hard to overcome.

Summer after the Ninth Grade and Pastor Art.

At the beginning of the summer, my older brother went to Oregon to live with my grandmother and her new husband on his farm near Albany. This was the Willamette River Valley where lots of farming activities were on-going, and help was needed, especially for Irrigation work.

My mother was pregnant with the last child of the family. Daddy told me I was to help my mother with all her activities, particularly with the washing of clothes and that I would have my allowance increased from ten cents per week to a dollar.

I, subsequently, did almost all the laundry and a lot of the other housework as well. I remember doing a lot of cleaning and dishwashing, something I had had to do a lot of the time anyway, and ironing of clothes was something I got pretty good at accomplishing.

It was during this summer that I was turning 14. Before that summer and during it, I became, somewhat of Pastor Art's fishing buddy. At one time he bought an old Ford car that, just previously, had its engine removed. He wanted this for his two adopted sons to play in, in their backyard. He came by and picked me up at my home Then asked me to steer the old car and operate the brakes as he towed it to his home. Afterward he invited me to go fishing with him out on Rolling Fork River. It was hot, and in the early part of the afternoon and thought it would be hot on the river. I declined, but I wish, now, I had accepted.

It was about this time that a church group picnic was held at Beaver's Bend State Park over the state line in Oklahoma.

It was decided that there would be a pie eating contest done without using hands and that Pastor Art and I would be the contestants. The pie was placed before us in a folding chair, and, on our knees, the contest began. I don't know who won, but again I was associated with Pastor Art in an activity.

During that summer, I was turning 14 and was getting ready to try for a driver's license. One time Art's wife, Shirley, invited me to drive their new Chrysler Desoto sedan. They previously had a '57 Chrysler two-door that had a mighty "Hemi" engine. This was before those engines became highly sought after for drag racing usage. After driving their new car (I had no problems and handled the car very well), Shirly found out that I did not yet have a driver's license and was surprised, but there was no harm done and I think that, as long I was with a licensed driver, it was permitted anyway.

There were other times when Art and I did go fishing and several of those times we went to Lake Greason. This Corp of Engineers Lake was constructed in 1947-1950 as a flood control on the Little Missouri River in west central Arkansas. The river later became the center of a flooding catastrophe when 7 inches of rain fell on its headwaters and, during the night, flooded the U.S. Parks Service campground at Albert Pike. Twenty (?) people were lost in the flood. The park has not since reopened. Our family had been to Albert Pike several times and it was a great place to swim and picnic. There was a deep pool at the bend in the river and the waters were clear and cool. There were large trees lining the banks on both sides, making the area very shady and cool. It was a haven for many people from near and far. The last time the family was there, I was about 15, Mom stepped out of the Women's room in her new swimsuit (it was the only one I ever remember her having) and she asked me to attach the last fastener at the top of the suit in the middle of her back. Feeling a little uncomfortable, I did that, and we proceeded to the swimming area.

Pastor Art and I went fishing another time in the spring of that year on Lake Greason. It was a Saturday, and we went quite a way down the lake to fish. I was at the front of the boat as we fished along a rocky shoreline which dropped off steeply into the water. I was in the front of the boat, and he was in the back. He began catching Crappie, while I wasn't getting a bite. Crappie are delicious perch-like fish that can grow to about five pounds for record fish. He was very pleased (understandably) with the fish and thought it amusing that he was catching them when I wasn't, but that's the way Crappie are, and you need to be lucky sometimes to find them.

At another time, as a part of a youth outing from the church, Pastor Art took several of us and his boat and we traveled north and west of Hot Springs to Lake Nimrod. As we drove Art talked with me about what I would like to do later in life as an adult. I told him that maybe becoming a radio and TV announcer might be interesting, and he was supportive of that. No one had ever talked to me about anything like that before.

We fished that day on Lake Nimrod, but this was in the early Spring and the weather turned overcast, cold, and windy. We had no luck fishing on the open water. Later we tried fishing in an inlet stream, but again, we had no luck.

We left that lake and headed back south toward Hot Springs, but detoured over to Lake Ouachita, which is a larger, but more protected lake just west of Hot Springs. We launched the boat and fished along an inlet, but still, although the lake was a more likely place to catch fish, we caught none, and I was starting to get hypothermia from all the exposure. At that point Art offered to rent a cabin for all of us to spend the night, rather than driving home. I'm sure he was tired, as I was, but I couldn't visualize the cabin as a warm and comfortable place to spend the night and we had no food, so I said I would rather go home. We did that.

Art also took my brother and I camping in early November at Lake Greason. Art provided all the camping gear and his new aluminum 14-foot boat and its 18 Horsepower Johnson outboard motor. This was the same boat as used in the previously described events, but it was new at this time, and this was one of its first times on the water. My brother and I had our cane poles, instead of rods and reels, and we must have been quite a sight fishing with them on the lake. Art never said a word about it as we proceeded with our fishing. We may have caught two white Sand Bass that day.

Prior to this adventure, I had found a baseball cap abandoned in the fairground's bleachers. It was black with the letter D (for De Queen?) on the front and may have been a team cap as used by the previous owner. When my older brother first saw it, he accused me of stealing it, even though there was absolutely no evidence to suggest that. The only motivation he could have had was jealousy. I was wearing the cap on the boat as we were fishing in the middle of the lake, when, again, in front of Art, he said: "You stole that cap!" I then reiterated that I had found it!

We spent the night in the tent and awoke to the permeating cold of the morning. To me, it was not fun. Art took the two Sand Bass we had caught and tried to cook them in a small pan on a camp stove fire. He used melted butter as oil, which was fine, but, when he tried to turn the filets over, they fell apart in the pan. They must have been fine to eat, but there wasn't much of them to share. It's hard not to like fresh white fish cooked in a pan over a camp stove.

Art and Shirley really worked a lot with the teenagers of the church and did many things to broaden our perspectives. During Christmas time, Shirley arranged to take a group to Texarkana to hear, for the first time, the oratorio "The Messiah." I had never heard of it. I didn't go to hear it, for whatever reason; I think I considered it a girl's outing, but I certainly, later, did become familiar with it. In fact, many years later, when I was attending computer science training at M.I.T. in Cambridge Mass. The entire class was taken to hear a professional presentation by, I think, The Hayden and Haydn Society in Boston, which was excellent in all aspects.

Shirley also provided our family with a phonograph recording of Tchaikovsky's Piano Concerto No. 1 to play on a newly acquired phonograph player gotten for the family with "S&H Green Stamps."

Art helped my older brother build a Tesla Coil for the high school fair during his senior year. That coil was quite a sensational exhibit for our school. He fired it up in our home, then blue and white electrical fire soon started coming out of the top into the air. This was all quite amazing.

He won First Place in the fair and was entered into the State Science Fair competition afterwards. The night before leaving for the fair, he had to rewind the copper wire of the vertical coil and spent all night doing so. He didn't win at the state fair.

Art was also interested in scientific matters and introduced the idea of stones, used to build the Pyramids, being floated into place using anti-gravity techniques. He was also interested in the religious theory of the Earth, being only 5,000 years old. That theory has been thoroughly discredited, but his faith made him hopeful that it could be true.

First Taste of Turkey

I must mention one other event that remains in my recollections: Thanksgiving Turkey! This was on Thanksgiving Day when I was 15 years old and playing on the high school football team.

Our last game of the season was always played against the Texarkana, Arkansas High School "Razorback Hogs." The location was alternated each year between the two home fields, this year it was in Texarkana. The weather had turned very cold with freezing temperatures and some possibilities of winter precipitation. The coaches provided some heat-generating balm for some of the players to put on the backfield players' hands to help keep them warm.

I don't remember the outcome of the game, typically Texarkana, being the larger school, won, but our team always put up a valiant fight and gave it everything we had.

After arriving with the team back in De Queen in the late afternoon, I walked from the school to Pastor Art and Shirley's home where they had invited my family for Thanksgiving dinner. There they were served the traditional turkey dinner, which we had never had before. I arrived after the dinner was completed to find that a turkey leg had been reserved for me. I found out then that I don't like turkey, especially the dark meat. I tried to eat it, but just couldn't.

In the recent years, I have had the opportunity to sample the white meat of a turkey that has been fried in peanut oil. That is delicious, especially with all the other side dishes that accompany it.

The Driving Test

In the State of Arkansas, and other surrounding states at that, it was possible to get a driver's license at the age of 14. I, of course, tried to get my license, more as a rite of passage than anything else. I got the instruction booklet and studied it well. When I went for the exam, I passed the written part passed the eye exam and was scheduled for the test drive with the examiner.

The first time I took the test the examiner told me to make an emergency stop; I took that to mean that there was some assumed mechanical problem. I slowed the car and pulled to the side of the road. Then I drove back to the courthouse and learned I had failed the test, but I was not told why.

The second time I took the driving test, I did the same with the emergency stop and again failed the test. Again, I was not told why I failed the test. The third time I took the test, the car engine died in downtown, on a main street, and the battery power was so low that I couldn't crank the engine. I wound up coasting (letting the car roll without the engine power) down the main street until I could turn on a side street that had a downslope and I could let the car build up enough speed to engage the clutch and let the momentum of the car turn over the engine. That worked and the engine started running.

I did the emergency stop the same as before, thinking I was doing the right thing. After that, after stopping at a Stop sign, the gear shift mechanism jammed, and I couldn't shift the gears. I knew what to do to fix the problem, but I had to get out, open the hood and pull up one of the gearshift levers by the steering column. I did that and drove back to the courthouse. I failed the test again, but the examiner commented that a car in better mechanical condition was needed.

Afterward, Daddy drove me home and tried to get me to tell him what had happened. I didn't want to talk about it, and I certainly was going to confide anything to him.

The next time I took the test, I had a new, and young, state trooper as the examiner, and he told me explicitly what he wanted to see with the emergency stop. As we rounded a corner down by the train depot, he suddenly said "Stop!" and I stopped almost immediately. I stalled the engine at the last stop sign, but that was the only issue, and I had, at last, passed the test and had my driver's license.

CHAPTER SEVEN
HIGH SCHOOL YEARS

Tenth Grade

Football practice started on the 20th day of August, which was still in the heat of the summer. The players were gathered in the gym and given their physical exams, this time the blood pressure readings for me and another boy were too high for ready acceptance. We were asked to sit for a while before our readings were rechecked; the next time we both passed and were cleared to play.

I was given some used shoes to wear by an assistant coach that were too long for my foot and the cleats were in front of the ball of my foot so that the shoe folded when I stepped. Despite the shoes, I was determined to play football and did the best I could; about a month later this was finally brought to the attention of the coach and some properly fitting shoes were found. I was used to being given no choice about anything at home and I certainly wasn't allowed to voice an opinion that something wasn't right; that mindset carried through to the football team coaches.

Practice began with "two-a-days" as before, and no water was allowed for the players during practice. One boy became overheated and fainted during the practice and I don't think he was allowed to continue with the team. I seemed to tolerate the situation as well as I had before. I consumed lots of liquids at home while I was recovering. The afternoon practice was better, as conditioning began to take hold.

The coach wanted me to play the interior lineman position of "Guard." I had never thought of that as a possibility, but I accepted it and began learning the position. I liked the action of "pulling" on some plays and blocking defensive players on the other side of the Center of the line as the ball carriers ran in that direction.

We had a night scrimmage, as a display for the local Boosters' Club, shortly before the school semester began. The coach lined us up across the field and went down the line introducing us. When he came to me, he pulled up the sleeve of my jersey exposing my forearm. He said: "I like a boy with big arms!" My forearms were developed, I'm sure, by all the cow milking I had been doing that required constant use of the forearm muscles. For the coach, liking my big arms, may have been the reason (partially) for him moving me to the Guard position.

I don't remember much of what happened that season, but one incident I do remember well. In a game played on the opposing team's field, on one play I was hit on my right leg when I had my foot planted in the ground and the leg could not bend away from the direction of the hit. This resulted in an injury to my knee and, many years later, I had to have surgery on that knee. The damage was painful, and it hurt every time I bent that knee. It didn't cripple me, however, and I did my best to keep playing. I didn't tell any of the coaches about it until about a month later when I was told to try some liniment on my knee. Surprisingly, a few days after starting the liniment, the knee stopped hurting. I'm sure it had to have affected my performance. Anyway, I survived and my passion for football was not diminished.

At the end of the season, it was the tradition of the schools to give out "Letter" jackets to the team players. These were nice jackets made of heavy felt-like material and lined with shiny satin-like material. The big letter "D" (for De Queen) was sewn on the outside on the left side and had stripes slanted across the left side (as viewed from the outside) one stripe was for each year that the player had "Lettered," meaning that player had sufficient playing time and impact on the field to be a valued player. Several of us "other" players didn't letter, but we still got jackets, albeit they were unlined (which I think was a bad decision on their parts). They still had the letter "D" on the outside, but without any stripes. I was glad to get it and that was my winter jacket.

Christmas Vacation from School

The town's athletic booster club had arranged for the team to be taken to the New Year's Day playing of the Cotton Bowl game in Dallas, Texas. Just as school was dismissed for the two-week holiday, I began feeling a rawness in my throat. This seemed to get worse with each passing day and I was soon very sick. The only treatment available to me was to gargle with hot salt water. This didn't work and I was feeling very achy and weak, passing the days by, mainly, sitting in a chair in the living room. New Year's Day came, and I knew there was no way I could make the trip, so I sat at home.

School began and I returned the first day, but I was so sick that I stayed home the next day. Finally, I was taken to the local clinic and received some medication. That seemed to work, and after the second day of absence, I was back in school. I talked to my mother, years afterward, and she was surprised to learn I had been so sick. She said that the clinic was available all along and I could have been taken at any time. I think a part of all of this was that I was very reluctant to bring up anything at home that would draw attention to myself as the consequences always seemed to be bad.

Other 10ᵗʰ Grade Experiences

One of my classes was Algebra II, in that class, one 11ᵗʰ grade girl began telling me, I should ask her for a date. I had no way of doing that as somewhat earlier Daddy had made his decree that I couldn't date until I was 16. I continue to believe that he did this as part of his way of showing authority over me and his dislike/hatred for me in general.

I, nevertheless, occasionally managed to evade the "No dating" directive. One of these occasions was a "Junior-Senior" hayride organized by the high school as part of the yearly traditions. One of the girls in the Junior Class asked me to go with her and arranged for another couple and her to pick me up at home on the appointed evening. I had not, of course, mentioned this to my parents and, when the car arrived, I quickly got inside, and we were gone.

The hayride started at the school and was accomplished by using two four-wheel trailers, which were covered with loose hay and towed behind two one-ton, flatbed trucks. The trailers had long tongues that connected them to the towing trucks.

We started out of the school and traveled along the gravel road leading to Johnson's Bridge. As we traveled, some of the boys, evidently, thought it was a good Idea to walk across the tongue to the back of the tow truck, and back as the trailers were in motion. Several of the boys did this and, luckily, no one fell off during this prank. If they had, they could have been badly hurt or killed by being run over by the trailer's undercarriage and, potently, by the following vehicle. I was not one of those as I and my date were making out while lying together in the hay on that trailer.

When we arrived back at school, one of the other students notified me that my parents were parked nearby. It became apparent that they had gone out looking for me and had trailed the hayride. I walked over and got in their car thinking I was going to catch holy hell by severe punishment. To my surprise, the only thing said was by my mother asking me if I had been one of those who had walked the tongue. I, while being greatly relieved, answered "No, I did not."

The Whippings

For years my daddy had been giving me whippings with his belt whenever he believed my supposed transgressions warranted it. In this 10th grade year, after school began for the second semester, he decided that I needed a whipping. I knew of nothing that I had supposedly done to be subjected to this, and he never gave a reason. I of course couldn't ask;

I was diligently doing everything at home I was supposed to be doing. He had me kneel over the edge of the bed while he lashed at me repeatedly with his doubled belt about 30 times. I was screaming" No, no, no" all the while this was going on. Afterward, the backs of my legs were black and blue from the deep bruising of the belt. These were clearly visible under my gym shorts at school.

The last of these whippings occurred later (I'm not sure of the exact timing, but I think it was in the Spring a year later after the whipping in January. I was outside the garage that the chicken laying house had become. Again, I don't know what set him off, but while I was standing there facing him, he yanked off his belt and began slashing at me as if I were an object that he just thoroughly hated. I just stood there and looked at him, not uttering a sound. Eventually he stopped and just looked at me, possibly realizing his trying to generate fear in me, was no longer working. He never tried to whip me again, but he devised other means to try to make my life uncomfortable.

I must mention this incident, and this may be as good a point, as any, to do so. When I was about 13 years old, Daddy had been taking a bath; this was during the winter months, because he was inside the dining room. He was in a wash tub that had been filled with about two inches of water, then hot water from a tea kettle, that had been heated on the kitchen stove, was added to the cold water, making it useable for bathing.

He had apparently decided he wanted to talk to me about whatever he had built up in his own mind that he thought I needed to hear. He called me in, and I saw that he was naked in the tub with his legs extended out onto the floor. A washcloth covered his genitals and there he proceeded to talk to me. I don't remember anything of what he said, but I was surely looking for a way to end that event quickly and get away from him.

At another time, my mother had cooked some liver as a main dish for our meal; this was just uncoated fried liver, with none of the side dishes that are often associated with it. The liver had a vile, excessively strong, taste that I couldn't eat, and I left it on my plate. My daddy observed this and told me I would have to sit right there at the table with the liver in front of me until I ate it, then he went to take his two-hour pre-swing shift nap. I sat right there during the whole time he was taking his nap and didn't touch the liver. He saw me when he got up and said," Alright, you can get up." I was surprised, as I was firmly committed to sitting there from then on if necessary. There was no way I could eat that liver.

I'll add at this point, because of the topic, that when I was in college, I returned home on a weekend and took a bath in the newly configured bathroom he had constructed. He had installed a water heater in the room, but it did not have a thermostat to control the burner. This burner also served as the heat source for the room, and this was a cold night. I lit the burner and took my bath, but not being really practiced in handling the accommodation, I left the burner on when I left.

The next morning, Daddy found the burner still on and accused me of trying to blow up the house. This was the most extreme conclusion he could have reached, but that was typical of his mentality. Later in life I would meet someone else with this same mentality. My experience with Daddy helped me to deal with that person, who later committed suicide.

Oregon in the Summers

After my Tenth-Grade school year ended in May, somehow, it was arranged that my older brother and I would go to Oregon to live with my grandmother and her husband Cecil and work on the local farms. We traveled by Greyhound buses up the western side of Arkansas to Kansas City, then across Kansas to Denver. The crossing of Kansas seemed interminable, with the bus driving very slowly as I watched the roadside pass through the lower window of the passenger door. Then it was on to Rock Springs, Wyoming, and Salt Lake City. Out of Salt Lake we headed into Idaho and arrived in Ontario, Oregon. There my Aunt Martha lived, and she met our bus.

Mt aunt wanted me to get off the bus, stay the summer with her and work locally at whatever jobs I could find. My older brother would travel on to Albany, Oregon, where my grandmother lived. A person-to-person phone call was made to Pastor Art's home in De Queen since my parents had no phone. After about 15 minutes, my parents came on the line and were relieved that the call was about a change in plans. It was stated that I was trying to "Get rich quick," and the change of plans was approved.

I spent a week with my aunt and her family, which included one of her husband's younger brothers who was older but close to my age. He had a green '56 Ford two-door with a V-8 engine. He liked to drive it fast, and I liked riding in it when he did. We traveled the highways and often drove across the Snake River border to the small town of Payette, Idaho, and others, where we would stop at the drive-in hamburger shops for a cola, then head back on the highways for home. On that Friday night, he took me to the "hardtop" auto races at the local dirt track and I loved it.

I could not find any work and after the end of the week, I was back on the bus headed west along the Columbia River to Portland, then south past Salem to Albany.

The weather in Oregon, in the Willamette River Valley region, was quite different from Arkansas. It was, at first in early June, like moving back to the conditions found in February – March in Arkansas, but nicer. Those first sunny days felt so comfortable that I just wanted to sleep when I sat down. Other times, it was the cold and rainy weather typical of the Northwest that was not so enjoyable.

The farm my grandmother and Cecil lived on had an old two-story house with a wood-fired cookstove in the kitchen and an attached very large woodshed that was filled with fir and other conifer trimmings that were easily split into cookstove sized pieces. A large space-heating wood stove stood in the living room. The piping for the hot water storage tank ran through the kitchen stove and worked very well. Outside the kitchen was a Bing Cherry tree; Bing Cherries are the ones used for making cherry pies.

My room (I had a separate room for the first time) was over the living room and my brother's room was over the kitchen. I had a clock radio near my bed and listened many times to "The Lucky Lager Dance Time" show when alone in my room. The windows did not have screens on them. On a night in later years, a large bat flew into my room in the middle of the night. I turned on the light, chased it back outside and was never bothered again.

The house was located on a slight corner in the gravel road that ran in front of it. Across the road was Cecil's barn, which was where the chickens and cats resided, and the cows were milked. I still have a picture of that old barn which was taken in later years by my aunt. In the barn sat an old automobile frame and engine, which had been left by the previous owner and was now covered with several layers of loose hay. The chickens laid their eggs in nests scattered across the barn and it always took some searching to find them all.

On his farm, Cecil grew alfalfa, vetch, tomatoes, strawberries (the big, sweet Northwest variety) cucumbers and other vegetables. The strawberries were often served by my grandmother with real cream separated by Cecil with the hand-cranked cream separator located in the kitchen. The cucumbers were picked daily to harvest the miniature "sweets" and were sold, with other vegetables, at the roadside by their home. Cecil would take the tomatoes into the town to sell to the grocery stores who would buy them, not all did.

Cecil had an old Ford ¾ ton pickup truck that he used on the farm and for trips into town. One peculiar feature of the truck was the foot pedal for the throttle: it was shaped like an inverted spoon and the floor around it provided no support for resting the driver's foot. Holding the foot pedal in one position for a constant speed seemed difficult to do. He also had a 1940's something Pontiac parked in a shed close to the road that hadn't been driven in years. In a later summer, that old car was revitalized by my aunt Martha's husband, who got the engine started and running again. I don't know if it was ever driven anywhere, certainly the license had expired a long time previously.

Finding Work

My first job was weeding beet sprouts; my grandmother heard that a farm in the area had a crew of workers out weeding a beet field and took me there to see if I could join them. Turned out that I could, but the crew was a long distance away from the start of the row I was given to begin weeding. I resolved that I would catch up to the crew and worked as fast as I could. Eventually, I was able to do that, and I stayed with the crew for the rest of the day. At the end of the day, the owner talked briefly with me about doing some other work, but nothing further came from that.

My next opportunity came shortly, when a neighbor farmer needed his beets weeded, and he had a lot of beets. In a field not far from my grandmother's home, a crew of young teenage workers were assembled, mostly they were from the city of Albany, rather than being local school children. Weeding requires the worker to follow the row on hands and knees, while using a small putty trowel to carefully dig out weed sprouts that had come up out of the ground with the beet sprouts. The soil was often muddy as well.

I showed up and the owner put me to work. I was told later that they were impressed with my work, which was described to me later, by "Monroe" the foreman, as "Nothing but assholes and elbows for that first half-day."

As we worked, I got to know the other teenagers and they came up with a nickname for me: "Sharky Arky," since I was from Arkansas and displayed some wit in our interchanges.

After the weeding was done, I was offered a full-time job by the farmer, "David," with the principal job being moving and resetting irrigation pipes in the many fields he had under irrigation. I was to be paid the princely sum of $1.00 per hour, which I was very glad to get. When my older brother found out what I was making, he was upset because he was only getting $0.90 per hour from the farmer he was working for.

My first task, however, was moving and staking back, the long canes that had grown in the areas between the rows of Boysen Berries. These canes had grown in those areas over the past year and staking them back was in preparation for rototilling as a method of cultivation of the soil. The canes were stiff and covered with sharp thorn-like stickers that were impossible to avoid. My arms were covered in healing scratches when I finished. The task took a week to complete, but I had worked at it steadily eight hours a day for the entire time. Did I say I was fourteen at the time?

The weather was changing from, mainly, cold light rain, to the clear and rainless pattern of the summer and we began the irrigation operations. Setting pipe in a field began with laying out the sixty-foot sections of sprinkler pipe along one edge of the field, then connecting those sprinkler pipes to the larger center pipes, which ran from the well. We used a "tree" that fit into the main line; this provided connections for distribution pipes which would then lay at right angles in both directions off the main line from the well. The first sprinkler pipe connected to the tree; the next sprinkler pipe connected to the first with a special fitting, and that pattern continued until the edge of the field was reached with the last sprinkler pipe. There could be 40 to 50 sprinkler pipes in a line across the field.

Resetting the pipe, after a 6 to 8-hour watering period, meant moving the mainline connection to the next station, then disconnecting the sprinkler pipes one-by-one, then carrying them 60 feet over to the next area and reconnecting them to the previously moved pipe. The ground under the pipes where they had just finished sprinkling was often muddy, making walking more difficult. But the ground under the next setting was dry and walking was easier.

When we weren't changing, or "moving" pipe, we were involved in whatever else was needed on the farm. Often that was working, with a small crew weeding the large peppermint fields (pigweeds and dog fennel seemed to be the worst offenders) using that ubiquitous farm tool: the hand-held hoe. The best one was small, light in weight and sharp on the blade. Carrying a file in the worker's pocket was always a good idea, as a sharp blade made cutting the weeds much easier. A hoe in use would need to be sharpened several times a day. Weeding with a crew wasn't bad work, as there was always conversation going on, and the weather was cool, usually in the 70's to low 80's, and the weeds, usually, weren't thick.

One of my earliest tasks was plowing a field of newly sprouted beets with a small Farmal Cub tractor that was equipped with the multi-plow and multi-row hydraulically activated cultivator. The driver (me) had to be very careful to maintain the proper clearance of just an inch, or two (at the most) between the plow and the beet seedlings. I spent that day cultivating those rows, and rows, beets back and forth, and back and forth, across the field.

At the end of the day, David arrived, but I was so intent on what I was doing that I didn't see him. As I approached the end of those rows, he gave a toot on the pickup's horn to give me an alert signal. As it turned out, I had plowed all the uncultivated rows and was re-plowing some rows that had been plowed about two weeks earlier, but that was okay, I had gotten the job done, plus some extra.

Swimming In the Santiam

I worked with another young man, and we got along great. In fact, one afternoon we decided to go swimming in the nearby Santiam River. We drove in his old car, a late '40's large luxury car, that had a fluid clutch system, that I don't think worked very well. The place where we went had no clear access to the river, as thick brush and trees were growing all along that point, and the bank was relatively steep. We, nonetheless, made our way through the brush and down the bank, then jumped into the relatively, swiftly flowing river. We were both strong swimmers and easily made it through the swift water to the rocky shoal on the other shore. We engaged in throwing rocks into the air and trying to hit them with another rock, then skipping lowly-thrown spinning rocks on the surface to see how many times we could get a single rock to skip. We finally swam back across the river and headed for home.

Bill The Softball Pitcher

The farmer family that my brother worked for had a son, "Bill," who was attending Oregon State College, which is in the regionally close city of Corvallis. There he was in the Alpha Gamma Rho Fraternity, which was/is, as I was led to understand, an agriculturally oriented fraternity. That was entirely appropriate for Bill's expected career, and being his parents' only child, stood to inherit the farm. The father, Mervin, was also the manager of the Dever-Connor Community softball team that played in the Men's Industrial League in nearby Albany on weekday nights. My brother and I were invited to go along with Bill and his parents to the games.

Bill was a pitcher and needed to practice some at home: I was drafted, instead of my older brother, to be the catcher while he threw his pitches on the grass of their home's front yard. This was fast-pitch softball and the ball travels at speeds close to 100 miles per hour. A baseball catcher's mitt couldn't be used, at least at that time, because the ball was too large, but that didn't matter, because I didn't have one. I would try to catch the ball in the webbing of a fielder's glove but doing that exactly was close to impossible. Most times the ball would strike in the palm of the glove and my hand would sting from the impact, but I was determined to stay with it, and I did. This, later, enabled me to play catcher and outfielder for the team.

At the games, I began to help the team with warm-up practice by hitting fly balls into the outfield. I did it in the same way I had used to hit balls in the field in front of our house in the years before: I would toss the ball up with one hand while holding the bat with the other, then grab the handle of the bat while the ball was in the air and swing at it as it fell toward the ground. This worked well then and still does today. I hit the balls up high into the outfield and some over the outfield fence. Some players would go there and call for me to hit some deep balls at them.

After the games, we would stop at a local ice cream shop for a treat, like a sundae or some other dish. I was said to often treat myself to my "usual" splendid "treats."

Waterskiing

Bill's family bought a runabout ski and fishing boat and equipped it with a powerful Scott-Attwater 40 Horsepower outboard engine. One Sunday, Bill, my brother, and I took it to the local access point on the Willamette River: a place called "Black Dog!" Why it was called that remains unknown to me, but it must have had a lot to do with the local lore of the community's founders. Access was through a pasture, after passing through a gate and driving along a dirt path. The beach was gravel, with a gravel bottom in the water. It was sufficient for a small boat launching, and was well-used later.

That first day, (in mid-June) the sky was overcast, it was raining lightly, and the air temperature was 55 degrees. The water temperature had to be much less and was, to a large degree, just melted snow. I had never skied before, but I was determined to try it, and I was successful. I fell several times, but that was just part of the learning process. I always got back on the skis and tried again. Later that summer, another man brought his smaller boat to the river, but it had a bigger motor and was faster (comparatively). I was offered a chance to ski behind this rig, and I took it. The speed of the boat was very fast, but I had no problems skiing behind it. I did notice that the small ripples on the water surface could be felt under my skis.

The Willamette River past the access point at Black Dog, seemed to be quite deep and the surface was reasonably smooth, but there were clear signs of water welling up from below, which would indicate that there were large boulders in the bottom. Were the river shallower, there could have been some "White water" rapids in that area.

In a later summer, a flotilla of large logs, was found to have lodged in a backflow area near the rocky beach. There were, seemingly, about 100 logs in this group, and I would think they represented a large investment by a logging company. It was surprising that no commercial operation came and moved those logs on toward the mill.

Peppermint Harvest

The wonderfully smelling peppermint growing in the fields changed at harvest time, from the fresh minty smell that clung to my jeans after moving the pipe and working in those fields, to a new and different smell with the harvest. The harvesting process begins with mowing the stalks, like hay would be mown back home. The mint stalks are then raked into rows like hay. But then, unlike hay, a chopper comes along and picks up the stalks from the rows, chops everything into very small pieces, and blows everything into a big tub that is being towed through the field behind the chopper. Once filled, the tubs are taken to a distillery where the tubs are sealed, then steam is introduced into the tubs.

This steam filters through the chopped mint and causes the oil in the peppermint to be mixed with the steam. The steam/oil mixture is then drawn off and the peppermint oil is separated from the steam.

Peppermint oil brings a very high price on the market. It is highly concentrated, and I was told (several times) that a single toothpick dipped in the oil, then swirled through a cake mix, would be enough to flavor the entire cake.

Once the chopped mix in the vats is fully processed, the vat is driven back to the field, where the mix is scattered in the fields that it came from. A result of all of this is that the countryside then smells like minty candy. The harvest and distilling process is a 24 hour a day operation and requires many workers. I never was asked to participate in the harvest operations, but I had other priorities and schedules anyway.

End of the Summer

In August, my parents and the rest of the family arrived, from Arkansas, at my grandmother's home. One of the main purposes of that was to transport my brother and I back home.

My brother and I were preparing for our usual night activities (probably going to a softball game) when my daddy said: "You haven't asked me yet!" That meant that he was apparently wanting to reassert his complete authority over us, and, from other forthcoming actions, particularly over me.

When the family was preparing to leave Oregon, my daddy told me that I was to sit right beside him in the front seat all the time as he drove back home. I have no idea what he had been thinking that would make that necessary, but whatever it was, it was something that he had built up in his own mind and I think that his objective was to, somehow, always keep me under his complete control. What he thought I might do otherwise is beyond my capability to reason through, but it certainly "set the stage" for happenings to follow.

I don't remember much about the trip home, fortunately there were no incidents with my daddy, and I was uncomfortable and uneasy sitting beside him, but resigned to make it through the trip. The route taken across the high desert of eastern Oregon was memorable for the terrain and colors of the sage vegetation. Next, it was on to Salt Lake City, then across eastern Utah into New Mexico to Albuquerque. Then on into The Panhandle of Texas and across the north border of Texas to southeastern Oklahoma. As we traveled into northeast Texas, I began to smell the weeds like what grew back home in Arkansas. Was that the smell of home? Maybe, but it was more like the smell of a place I really didn't want to be.

In Oregon, I had used some of my earnings to buy clothes that I could wear to school. Then, as school started, I used my savings to buy my schoolbooks, never thinking that my parents should have borne those costs. The family was hard pressed to meet the basic needs of the family with the income they had from my daddy's work, but I will also mention at this point that, despite the limited family income and the family's needs, a strict 10 % of that income was given to the church.

Church Matters

It was in the Spring of my high school sophomore year that Pastor Art made the announcement that he was not meeting his goals in the church, and it was time for him, and his family, to move on. I also suspect that at some point during that Spring, after Pastor Art had observed many happenings in my family and, from his very positive, personal interactions with me, thought that I wasn't being treated fairly, or in any way how a teenager should be handled. I believe he made a point of talking to my daddy about all of this and how some changes needed to be made. This, of course, was completely intolerable to my daddy, and for him to be criticized by a preacher made it even worse. I suspect there was a heated discussion between my daddy and Pastor Art, and I was the problem, it could never be him. This, in my view, is what led Pastor Art to want to leave the church.

On night after church, in the parking lot as we were getting ready to leave, my daddy walked up to me and suddenly, without saying a word he grabbed me around my throat as if he was going to chock me. I don't know how far he was thinking he would take that, but I just stood there not resisting and he eventually released his grip. I had no idea what it was that caused him to do that, other than he just hated me and my existence, but the fact that it happened at the church leads me to believe it was associated with all the recent happenings with Pastor Art.

At another time close to the previous event, but after it, in the Spring probably, a Sunday Evening church service was under way and the congregation was standing while singing one of the hymns. I was across the aisle behind my daddy when I noticed him looking over and back at me with a strange look. He, shortly, came across the aisle to stand beside me and ordered that I sing louder. Apparently, the lack of enthusiasm of the congregation would be solved, in his mind, by me singing louder.

At home it was mandatory that everyone participate in nightly "Devotionals" led by my mother. The pattern that these took was for all of us to read a passage from the Bible and we started in Genisis and read the passages progressively each night. I think we read the Bible through four times. I must confess that the last time through some of the books of the Old Testament, I understood the passages that got sexually explicit. On such passage had the phrase "Laying between thy breasts," or something like that. That was interesting to a teenaged boy.

After reading, we had to kneel on the fronts of our chairs and each of us, in turn, would say a prayer. This was all done aloud for all to hear and meant having to make up something to say (and "pray") about. I hated it. This went on nightly into my junior year in high school and I'm sure my building resistance to all of this, although not voiced, was taken as a rebellion against Daddy's authority.

I had also been made to participate in the Bible Memory Association program, which meant that each week I had to memorize preselected long passages from the Bible, then recite them on Saturday to a monitor. I had to spend hours and hours during the week doing this. I absolutely hated it but continued with the efforts until near the end. Participants were given reading books as rewards; typically, these were easily read books about "The Sugar Creek Gang" of kids and their adventures.

I didn't finish the program, as my older brother had the previous year and he had been awarded a week in the summer at "Miracle Camp" in Ringold, Louisiana. A requirement to enter the camp was, reportedly, being able upon arrival to recite 50 verses memorized from the course. I was deathly afraid of failing that requirement. My older brother also didn't attend the camp that year or ever again.

There was an attempt by my daddy and some others to try to increase church attendance from the local townspeople. It was decreed by Daddy that, on a Saturday, he, my older brother, and I would canvass the town, knocking on doors and giving our message to the people. We were to individually go out into the town to do this. Of course, I was extremely reluctant. I had to knock on doors, then say things I didn't mean and try to make the best of it.

One lady I talked with invited me inside; I'm sure she could easily detect my unease and lack of sincerity in what I was saying, but she was kind and pretended not to perceive all of that. My brother and I later met near the center of town and were ready to be done with all of this, but about that time,

Daddy showed up and ordered us back out into the town. There was no increase in attendance at our church afterward.

My high School Junior Year

In the fall season this year my older brother left for college in September and went out of state to Cedarville, Ohio. Why this was chosen, I really don't have a good reason for except that Cedarville College was a "Christian" school. He has told me that he had applied for the Merchant Marine Academy and thought that a year in college would help gain the congressional appointment. Shortly after my brother's departure, my daddy met me out in the front yard under the sweet gum tree and, without any preceding discussion, said "I'm not going to help you with college."

It wasn't long after that, in the late winter or early spring, that he told me "If you don't do everything, I tell you to do, exactly as I say to do it, you will have to leave home!" It shortly came to pass (predictably, I think) that one night he had had enough. He called me downstairs about 10:30 and told me that I was going to have to leave. Thoughts were going through my head about where I could go, I really had no Idea. I thought of my grandmother in Oregon, but that would require asking her permission and a bus trip out there for starters.

Just then my mother emerged from the bedroom crying and, as she said it, she told me to go back upstairs and my daddy to come back to their bed. He did that, and I went back upstairs, and nothing else about that was ever said until years later in a discussion with my mother.

Home Study Electronics Course.

Daddy had embarked upon a home study electronics course during my 10th grade year, and he diligently pursued it. He spent many late nights studying at a large mahogany (like) table located upstairs in the boy's bedroom. He also converted the laying area in the chicken laying house into a study/laboratory where he could do the practical parts of the course. The end-of-course training session was to be completed in the training company's facility in Kentucky or Ohio, I don't know which. That time came, during the spring of my 11th grade school year that he took a leave of absence from his work and prepared to leave, driving the car alone all the way.

On the day he left, it was a Saturday, and I was working at the local Piggly Wiggly grocery store. He stopped by to talk to me before he left, but I didn't want to talk with him, or even be in his presence. He came up to me when I was outside and stopped me as I was returning inside the store. He told me I would have to take care of everything, including handling all the cows in his place while he was gone. This was after the night he had tried to expel me from his home. I took care of all of the outside animal care and other matters during his absence and there was no issue with any of it. There was also no acknowledgement, or anything else from him, when he returned.

Car Mileage

During the late winter months, when basketball was still in season, I came home one night after a local game and parked the car in the garage. I subsequently noticed that my daddy had just gone into the garage and returned. Apparently, he had gone out to check the mileage and then told me I had driven too many miles to just go to the school gym and return. Turns out, I had taken another player, who lived about a half mile from the school to his home, before coming home.

I thought, "Alright, I can play that game" and thereafter, whenever I wanted to drive some extra miles, I simply disconnected the speedometer. He never caught on and never raised the issue again. I think it is important to relate that he never gave any instructions, or limitations on how and where I was to use the car, so I relied on what we did in Oregon: which was to cruise the drive-ins after the softball games. I confess to doing some wild things with friends, but it was never anything beyond good fun and was always safely done.

Epiphany

That spring, and I was outside close to the garage, when, despite all the negativity and hate I had received at home, I literally said to myself: "I'm a good person." People like me, I do good work, I am a good athlete and a team player, etc., etc. I had no problems, except at home with my daddy.

Junior Year Return to School and Sports

The end of the summer work for me needed to be just before the 20th of August; that was because football practice at my high school, and for all the schools in my conference began on that date. My return to school to start that practice turned out to be quite an adventure.

I was not looking forward to another bus ride across the western United States, this time being west to east. A travel agent was consulted, and it was determined that I could work a few days longer and make enough money to offset the cost of flying over the cost of a bus ride. I chose to do that, and the tickets were purchased for flights from Portland to Denver, and from Denver to Kansas City. I could then ride the Kansas City Southern Railroad to De Queen. A transfer from the Kansas City Airport to the train station was to be by city bus.

On the appointed morning, my aunt, who was married to my Uncle Murray, and my grandmother drove me to Portland/ Vancouver Airport. There I boarded the airplane and found my seat. On the food tray in front of me was a small package containing four cigarettes. I didn't even think about trying to smoke them but did take them with me later.

The plane was a DC-7 with four big radial engines and probably was a derivative of the B-17 Flying Fortresses of World War II. We took off and climbed out of the Portland area. As we neared cruising altitude an announcement came over the PA system that the noises we were hearing was the shifting of the superchargers. That was comforting I guess, but truth be known, I had not noticed the noises prior to the announcement. The rest of the flight was uneventful and landed in Denver.

I made my connection for the next flight and once we were at cruising altitude (I don't think we were as high as the flight over the Rocky Mountains); I looked out and saw the extended flat lands that make up Kansas; they seemed to have no boundaries.

Once out of Kansas City Airport (this was the old airport close to downtown) I saw a taxi at the curb and asked about going to the train station. The driver was more than happy to take me there and the fare was just a few dollars. That saved me the adventure(?) of trying to find the bus and figuring out the route and the connections.

There was a long wait in the station for the train to begin boarding. Afterward, as the train began to pull out of the station, when I had not felt the beginning motion of the train passenger car, I looked out and saw the terminal dock moving past my window and thought it was moving and the train was standing still. It was a very strange feeling, but soon I saw what was really happening.

The train ran on through the night and the next morning was nearing the area of De Queen. One of the first things I noticed was the smell of the vegetation, particularly, a whitish weed that I could see along the track. Upon arrival in De Queen there was no one there to meet me, so, after claiming my luggage, I asked a taxi driver to take me home. On the way we began to chat, and I told him I was returning home to start football practice. His comment was that he sure didn't want me to hit him - meaning when making a football play.

As we were leaving the city limits, I saw my mother and the rest of the children driving toward town on their way to pick me up, but, of course, they were very late. They saw me and the taxi driver stopped and let me out. He didn't charge me the fare, which he should have and that was appreciated.

Football Season

Preseason practice this year was held at the Sevier County Fairgrounds, which afforded a better and grassier field than before. I was again playing the Guard position on the 2nd string offense, but primarily was playing on the defensive team against the 1st string offense in practice. In the games, I played a lot in the defenses, mostly at linebacker. Sometimes I was also on the "Kickoff" team and my assignment was to go to the ball carrier to try to make the stopping tackle. In a game against Hot Springs High School, which was out of our conference, I was particularly pleased to be selected for the starting Kickoff team. In recent years, my older brother told me that he and my daddy had attended that game, but I had no recollection of that and am not sure I ever knew it.

The local newspaper, "The De Queen Bee," ran weekly pictures of various players and about mid-season my picture was published. The write-up described me as a "Defender," but also stated that I had made a strong bid for "Starting' Status at the Guard position. I never knew that and thought the guy playing there was a pretty good player. He was certainly older and bigger than I was. But it was okay with me not to be starting in the offense, I was getting a lot of playing time on the defense.

About mid-season, the coaches needed players to run a single-wing offense for the first team defense to practice against. I was selected to play in the backfield at the "Fullback" position. The assistant coach was playing quarterback. They gave me the ball in the backfield, and I started "ripping off long-gainers" against the defense. This was reported afterward in the newspaper. After that afternoon, I was no longer a lineman and was installed as a full-time offensive backfield player. Some special "Inside Belly Series" offensive plays were even adopted to utilize my running abilities through the defenses.

In one practice, I was running against the first team defense and was given the ball to run into the right side of the defense. As I was running, three of the biggest and toughest players hit me in succession trying to make a tackle. After each hit, I regained my balance and ran on. The coach stopped play and told his defense that sometimes you run into a ball carrier that doesn't go down on the first hit, and they had to do a better job of tackling.

In one practice later, I was given the ball to carry on an inside running play between the Center and the Left Guard. As I ran into the line, I felt, and saw, an opposing player hit me around the knees and then went to the ground as I ran on.

It turned out that the player suffered a spinal fracture and wound up being in the hospital in a body cast for a couple of months. I took no pleasure from the fact that the contact resulted in an injury to the other player, but I felt that the result was caused by playing a game in which inherent risks exist. I really felt no need to visit the player in the hospital, but it was brought to my attention that the player thought I should have come to see him when I hadn't. I subsequently made a visit to the hospital and what I saw was not pretty. He was in a cast from his waist to his neck in a bed and had to have been miserable. That player played no more football and was said to have "soft" bones.

I also sustained an injury in practice one afternoon close to mid-season. The players all wore metal cleats on their shoes to help with traction in the dirt of the fields. These were about ¾ inch long. During one play my hand wound up on the ground and another player stepped on the back of it causing a big gash in the flesh just behind my right ring finger and the middle finger next to it.

I returned to the huddle and said "Coach, I've got a problem, then showed the gash between my fingers. I was sent to the showers and a couple of other players left the practice also and then took me to the local clinic, where the wound was cleansed and sewn up with sutures.

Two days later, I suited up for the game that Friday night and the coaches found a rubber pad that they taped to the back of my hand and fingers. I played the game as usual, but at one point I had gotten hit on the hand, and it stung a bit with the pain. The coaches looked at it and said, "You're okay" and sent me back into the game. I still have the scar and can see where the stitches were taken.

In one game I was instructed to change jerseys with another player, because numbers were assigned according to positions played. My regular number was for a lineman and the other player was a substitute backfield player. Some didn't notify the PA announcer calling the game and, all during the game, the other player was given credit for the plays that I ran.

In a subsequent game with Mena, Arkansas, the offense on the field, had moved the ball down close to the goal line, when the head coach sent me into the game – at Fullback. The quarterback saw the coach's purpose and called a play that gave me the ball and ran it into an off-tackle direction into the line. We ran the play, I was given the ball and crossed the goal line untouched, but I didn't know what to do after that, so I ran on a bit further and eventually was tackled deep in the end zone. That scored the Touchdown, and I was given credit for scoring – my one and only offensive score.

In one home game I was instructed to change jerseys with another player, because numbers were assigned according to positions played. My regular number was for a lineman and the other player was a substitute backfield player. Someone didn't notify the PA announcer calling the game and, all during the game, the other player was given credit for the plays that I ran.

I did manage to score an additional touchdown that year but did it on defense. We were playing the Eastern Arkansas team from De Witt, Arkansas for the first of a multi-year two-game arrangement to compare teams from equal-sized towns in two different regions. We played on their field, and, during the game, their team was backed up near their own goal line: they decided to run a pitchout play to my side of the defensive line. That was a good plan except for the fumble which occurred when the pitchout back failed to catch the ball pitched by the quarterback. That ball fell on the ground in their end zone, and I quickly covered it. That gave my team a touchdown and six points. The next day, in the Arkansas Gazette (the Little Rock newspaper) that play was credited to a star running back on our team, which figures, I guess.

After the game ended, the team bus was driven to Little Rock to spend the night, and the next day, to attend a college game between The University of Arkansas Razorbacks from Fayetteville and the Red Raiders of Texas Tech from Abilene. I had no idea this was in the offing before we left home to play the game, but it turned out to be a very good experience.

The stadium was huge, in my experience, and the pageantry was amazing. The Texas Tech Masked "Red Raider" rode onto the field on a black horse and carrying a team flag. The horse's hooves also went through the surface of the end zone and indicated, to me, that the area was too wet for ideal conditions. The bands were playing, and it was a spectacle never witnessed by myself and, I'm sure, my teammates.

The Arkansas band trumpets occasionally played the calvary bugle call "Charge!" But they did it in sets of three with each iteration beginning an octave higher than the last. It was thrilling (to me) to hear it.

Don't remember who won the game, as if that mattered…

The final game of the season was, again, the traditional game with Texarkana, this time in De Queen. The weather had turned cold and overcast, with a cool north wind. The coaches had formed teams using all the seniors on our team to give them all a chance to play in their last high school game.

In the last quarter, however, the Texarkana team was moving down the field and nearing scoring territory. The head coach called me up and told me to go play outside linebacker, because Texarkana was making some advancing plays by running outside the line on that side. When I got on the field, however, one of the other players who had been playing as an inside linebacker asked me to let him play there and for me to take the inside linebacker position. I said "Okay" and we continued to play. I was able to penetrate the line and force the other team to run wider than they had intended, but we were, ultimately, unable to prevent them from scoring. I played the next defensive series at inside linebacker as well, but we ended up losing the game, as usual.

Basketball

Prior to the start of the basketball season, and after the end of the football scheduled games, the football players who would be playing the next year were doing a drill called "Bull in the Ring." In this drill the players stand in a circle with one player in the middle. One at a time, and in no particular order, one player would charge at the player in the center and deliver a body hit on that player. The player in the center would, of course, try to fend off the hit and not be knocked out of position.

I was in the center when a particularly large player, (actually, a year younger, but larger than me) charged. I absorbed the blow with my shoulder, but I felt a snapping sensation around my right collarbone and I'm sure it was broken. I, nevertheless, continued the drill and never mentioned the condition to my coaches or my parents.

Basketball

With the start of basketball, I began to attend pre-season practices. Basketball practice had already begun before the end of football season and several times I finished football practice then returned to the school for early basketball practices). Other players who were playing football didn't attend those early practices, but I felt compelled to do it and was able to absorb the physical requirements just fine.

The broken collarbone presented me with some uncomfortable pain in my shoulder, but this lessened and disappeared in the space of two months and I suffered no continuing discomfort in the area.

Sports banquet

In the spring of this year, April I believe, a sports banquet was organized and held in the school cafeteria on a weekday evening. Players were to invite their fathers to attend with them. I attended alone, never thinking that Daddy might want to attend; I certainly wasn't looking for any father/son time with him. He later made a comment that he had not been invited. That indicates to me that he had no concept of the effect of what he was doing at home, but, of course, he, in his own mind, could never have done anything wrong and he had a God-given right to do it.

The food at the banquet was quite good. The main course was fried chicken; this turned out to be fried chicken like I had never eaten before; it was delicious. We were served half of a chicken, floured and deep fried like fried chicken restaurants serve today. I can still taste it...

Glee Club

This was a choral group in school that was an actual voluntary club, but conducted in a very professional manner, like an instrumental band. It was called "The Glee Club" and met on school mornings prior to the first class. This was all a very good experience for me. We first performed a Spring concert one evening in the choir loft of the local Methodists Church. The boys all wore white sports jackets, and the girls wore nice dresses. I borrowed a sport coat from a classmate: the same one, ironically, that I had a fight with in the Ninth Grade. I greatly appreciated the loan as there was no way I could have gotten one at home. One song we sang was "All in an April Evening," which I thought (and still do) was almost magical in its sounds and melodies.

The club traveled on an overnight trip to a mid-state college for a gathering of choirs from other schools around the state. At the event there was a group rehearsal during the day, then a concert of selected groups at night. Our group was featured during the evening session.

For our housing, we were told to bring a set of sheets for our bedding. I did that and borrowed a neighbor's small briefcase to carry them, but that was all I brought: no change of clothes, no concert wear, no toiletries, nothing. I should never have been allowed to leave home with just the sheets. Luckily, one of the college men, with whom I stayed, perceived the situation, and outfitted me in one of his shirts and a sports coat for the concert. The shirt had a Chinese collar (in fashion at the time) and I felt quite good in my loaned outfit.

The choir also, later, attended the state competition in Hot Springs. We traveled in a school bus and on the way, I started to get very sick to my stomach. The pain grew and grew, until I had to vomit. To not contaminate the inside of the bus, I stuck my head outside the window of the traveling bus and let go. The result, later, was a smear of strains on the side of the bus that stayed there for the rest of the trip. I also, later, developed diarrhea and had to be taken to a doctor.

The choir director paid for the prescription and had me stay in a room that had been rented as a "refreshing" room for the girls. I rested for the rest of the afternoon. She, later, asked to be paid back for that prescription, which had been for some paregoric (a commonly used medicine for my symptoms). When I paid her later, she looked at me and said, "This is your money, isn't it." I nodded, "Yes," and it was. I had not asked for money from my parents as I had not asked for any money for some time. I had the money I had saved in Oregon, from which I bought my clothes, my schoolbooks, my lunches, and any other needs I had. I also worked in a local grocery store on Saturdays for most of the year.

When I returned home from the trip, I found out the entire family had come down with the same illness that day. And my daddy had procured a large bottle of Paregoric for the entire family. It was said that the contaminated food came from a church supper that was the night before, but I believe it was from some contaminated food we all had for breakfast. My situation was the most difficult, especially for me, of the entire family.

Valentine's Carnival.

Various fund-raising events were held during the school year, These, I found out later, were to help finance a post-graduation trip to New Orleans for the senior class. One of these was a Valentine's Carnival that was held in the school auditorium. The auditorium itself was a semi-converted basketball court with a stage. In one of the door-wells a penny-pitching booth had been set up and it was being run by a senior girl, who was the sister of one of the boys in my class. The object of the game was to pitch pennies, one at a time and try to land them in a coffee can about 8 feet from the throwing line. I stepped up and repeatedly tossed my pennies into the can. The girl looked at me in amazement, and I guess she got a good look at me for the first time.

A day, or so, later I got word from a girl in my Algebra II class that this "Penny Pitching Booth" girl had a "crush" on me. We met shortly thereafter, and she and I spent some casual time together. She taught me how to dance (somewhat, as best I could ever be taught) at a school evening function. I knew, however, that I could never "date" her the way others in the school, with their own cars, and money could. So, we drifted apart towards the end of the school year.

A Confidential Chat

During this year in school, I think it was in the fall during football season, I was talking with two of the senior girls in the library. I don't remember the topic of the conversation, or how it drifted to this subject, but one of the girls told me

I was one of the "best boys" in the school. Well, this greatly (quite understandably I think) helped my self-esteem and I, later, told a friend of mine who I played football with, as we waited for a ride home after practice, about the conversation.

The next day, I heard that he had spread the word of our conversation around the school. Why did he do that? I don't know, I certainly didn't appreciate it. Ultimately, this betrayal really didn't affect our friendship, and we had some future adventures together.

The point in mentioning this is that it is evidence of my likability and esteem in the eyes of others, this helped me form a better image of myself than the one I was getting at home.

Oregon II

School ended and I prepared to leave on another long bus trip to Oregon. This time I had a job with David waiting for me on arrival. The bus trip was arranged Through Continental Trailways rather than Greyhound and it took a different route from Fort Smith which took me across the southern route into California, then into Bakersfield, Sacramento and on into northern California. We approached Mount Shasta in the afternoon, and I marveled at how gigantic (and white) it was. Then it was into southern Oregon, up the Cascade Mountain Range and, finally, arriving in Albany. Don't remember much more about the journey, but that, with all things considered, is what you want on a bus trip.

The summer was spent moving Irrigation pipe, hoeing weeds and whatever else needed to be done on the farm. One of those things was being instructed to build a tailgate for a flatbed Ford truck that would later be used for hauling beets to the cannery in Salem. My employer, David, had me go to the closest nearby town, Jefferson, and buy the carriage bolts necessary for assembling the gate out of two-by-four and one-by-four lumber. I built the gate, and David was very pleased that I had managed to keep it "square" and assembled it well.

David had bought a "beet puller" machine, with which he and I were going to harvest table beets in various fields on area farms. He had beet fields of his own to harvest also. This "puller" was an amazing machine that sent a plow under the row of ripe beets, then grabbed the upper beet stalks and pulled them out of the ground. The pulled plants were then passed on to a set of rotating "knives" that cut off the upper stalks leaving the beet roots to fall onto a conveyor, on which they were lofted over to a trailing wagon, or truck and dropped into its cargo area. It was a one row at a time operation and the puller was towed by a tractor and powered by the PTO (Power Take Off) from the tractor transmission. Before beginning work, it was desired by David to devise a means of engaging the puller conveyor only at desired times. This was to allow for the trailing truck to position itself under the moving puller's conveyor before allowing the beets to be moved up the conveyor to be dumped in the truck. David engaged me in the design phase, and we used my algebra training to calculate the length of a new V-belt that ran over three pulleys. One of those pulleys was mounted on a moveable arm and, when engaged (starting the conveyor), it was held in place by being "over-centered" past the tightest position of the belt. With just one minor adjustment, the assembly worked as desired.

My Initial job was to drive the tractor, which I found out was not a simple as it would seem. The fields weren't all level, and some had some significant slopes onto which the pulling rig had to be properly positioned to continue pulling beets. When a slope was encountered the rig would shift downhill despite the position of the tractor in the center of the row. The puller operator could do some minor compensation to keep the rig in the center of the row, but we found out very quickly that more adjustment than what was available was needed. I determined that I could drive the tractor on the uphill side of the row just beside the next row and give the plow operator the means to keep the plow centered. Additional vigilance was required of me as I drove, but that was okay, as that was a learning experience, and the adjustment was required for successful team operation.

I also had to make the turn-around moves at the end of the row and properly position the puller at the beginning of the next row to be pulled. I tried to do that with as few moves as necessary and as quickly as possible, and I think I was pretty good at it. On one of those turn-around moves when we first began pulling, on the first field. I pulled the tractor-puller assembly out of the row and out of the way of the trailing wagon which had been collecting the beets. That wagon also had a conveyor that would unload the newly pulled beets onto a truck, and it stuck out into the air behind the trailer. The top of the puller conveyor and the top of the wagon conveyor were about the same. As the wagon, driven by "Monroe," was pulling past the puller, David saw that the conveyors would not clear each other and there could be a bad accident if they collided. I immediately saw the same and put the tractor in gear pulling my conveyor clear of the other. I don't think Monroe even knew what happened as the accident was avoided, but I made sure on all future end-of-row moves to make sure the was ample clearance between the two conveyors.

David and I pulled many fields of beets that summer, and we kept the puller well maintained and lubricated.

One mid-summer afternoon, after pulling and filling two trucks with beets, it was decided that I would drive one of the loaded trucks to the cannery and Monroe would drive the other. There were, probably, 4-6 thousand pounds of beets on each truck, but Monroe was driving the Ford with the big V-8 engine, and I was driving an old GMC with its straight 6 engine. To add to the stress of the situation, I didn't know where the cannery was in the city of Salem. Out on the highway the other truck pulled away, but as we neared Salem, he slowed down enough for me to catch him as we drove through the downtown city streets.

We reached the cannery, and my truck was put on a platform that tilted the entire truck up to about a 45-degree angle to dump the beets out of the back. We returned home after making the trip safely and I was relieved. Later Monroe teased me about being far behind in the country, but very close in the city. That was okay with me as I reasoned that he might not have realized that I didn't know where we were going.

Timber Carnival.

A big celebration occurred each summer in Albany, to celebrate the timber industry in the area, called (naturally) The Timber Carnival. This carnival featured many contests of lumbering skills including Pole climbing, sawing, and chopping and,

the most difficult of all: Log Rolling. The townspeople
and merchants of the city, of course, supported the event
and everyone was supposed to get a timber carnival badge,
which cost a few bucks, but was highly affordable. I went
into town on a Saturday and needed a haircut, so I stopped
at a shop downtown. That day there were roving carnival
marshals looking for people without a badge to "arrest" and
bring before a Carnival Magistrate who had set up court in
the middle of town. I didn't have a badge and was in the
barber chair with the barber drape around my neck when
the marshals showed up. They pulled me out of the chair,
still wearing the cloth around my neck before the carnival"
Judge." Who sentenced to buy a carnival badge right there. I
bought the badge and made it back to the barber chair where
the haircut resumed.

Another feature of the carnival was the giving of airplane
rides, for a fee, of course. David, the man I worked with and
for, knew from our conversation that I had an interest in
airplanes and that I had never ridden in one. He volunteered
to pay for us to go for a ride in one of those planes and, on
a Saturday morning, we went flying. The plane was a single
engine low-wing craft with four seats, and I was allowed to sit
in the right front seat with the flight controls and instruments
in front of me. At no time was I invited, however, nor did
I try to use the controls; that was fine as I was taking in
the experience. We flew out over David's farming area and
returned to the airport. I greatly appreciated the gift and
years later, in the '70's, I completed training and obtained a
private pilot's license.

CHAPTER EIGHT
SENIOR YEAR AND
AFTERWARD.

Senior Year Sports

Football practice began (again) in August, and I was hoping to play in the backfield as I had been doing when the previous season ended when I was a junior. I told that to the head coach, but he had other priorities. He told me he wanted me to play the Right Tackle position in the offensive line, so I accepted that and began working to learn the position. That wasn't hard as I had previously been playing the Guard position. I wore the Jersey Number 76, designating a "tackle" player in the numbering system; Centers were 50's, Guards were 60's, tackles were 70' and ends were 80's; other numbers were designated for the "backfield." I also became the kickoff specialist for the team and did that for the entire season.

We didn't have enough players to have an "Offense" and "Defense" team, so many of us played both ways, which meant that we played the entire game. That was fine, and we thought nothing of it; we were just glad to be in the game and contributing what we could.

Practices were long, and conducted without any water to drink, even during the hot days of late August and into October: that was just the way it was. To add to this, we always ran "wind

Sprints" at the end of practice. These sprints were run with increasing yardage intervals for "down and back" sprints: first 25 yards, then 40 yards, then 50 yards and, sometimes, 100 yards.

At the end of one practice on an August afternoon, in midfield at the end of a 50-yard sprint, the head coach told me to go sit down on the nearby opposing team bench. I was unsure of what this meant, and I asked him "What did I do?" His reply was that I had run that one: meaning that I had expended some effort, and he was satisfied with my effort, while he wasn't satisfied with the others. Gradually more and more players were sent to join me.

At the end of one practice, on a particularly hot day, we were given handfuls of ice to suck on; that was good, but it only happened once. I remember, during the season's practices, catching the sweat coming off my face with my tongue to moisten my mouth; really, I liked the salty taste, and it helped me get through the practices. I'm told that a few years later all the denial of water practices changed, and players could have all the water they wanted during practices. This was, as I understand, good medical practice as dehydration can be dangerous.

Season Games

Early in the season we played against the team from Mena, Arkansas: a town about 45 miles north of De Queen. During the last part of that game, after a kickoff and as I was running down the field, an opposing player attempted to block me and, really, was trying to tackle me, which was illegal. He wrapped himself around my legs to "hold" me. I responded by hitting him with my fist. A referee saw this, threw a flag, and ejected both of us from the game. The next day I was elected President of my senior class.

During the game we played against Arkadelphia, I scanned the stands and saw my supposed girlfriend sitting with another guy, apparently on a date. I couldn't do anything about that from the field, but I could do something about blocking the opposing player in front of me, and for the rest of the game I gave it everything I had. The opposing team finally moved a bigger guy, who had been playing the "Nose Tackle" position over to play in front of me. I blocked him just as I had been blocking the other player. In the end, we lost the game with a score of 7 to 6.

After the game, the opposing players sought me out and as I was going into the locker room, several came up to me and told me "76 you played a whale of a game!" I nodded my acceptance and thanks for the remarks, but I was upset about the "girl" situation. It is interesting to note that for the rest of the season, opposing teams always played a defense alignment that had no one directly opposing me on the line of scrimmage. We would practice against the expected defense, then in the game they would line up in the 5-4 defense with no one directly in front of me. I was very frustrated by that during those games and really didn't know which player behind the line of scrimmage to try to block.

We played one of our last games against our archrival "Nashville," a town about 40 miles to the east of De Queen.

Their team ran the "Single Wing" offensive alignment that favors running plays to their right. I was playing defensive end on the opposite side of the formation, partly because I could pursue plays on the opposite side of the field, and I was good at stopping scrimmage plays running directly at me. As the game progressed, I made many tackles on both sides of the field and was told later that the PA announcer had often given my name as the tackler by saying: "Caplinger makes the stop, on the right side" then, "Caplinger makes the stop on the left side."

Toward the end of the game, after trying several counter-plays in my direction, they ran another. This time the offensive player on the line grabbed my ankle in an illegal "holding" move as I ran past him; the referees didn't see it and the result was a touchdown for them. Later, after the game and at our post-game meal, the coach came over, sat down at my table, and told me that I had stopped them many times when they would have, otherwise, gone "all the way" and scored. I didn't tell him about being held on that last scoring play; maybe I should have, but it wouldn't have made any difference.

Another game late in the season was an "away" game with the team from Ashdown High School. Ashdown was a town located about 35 miles south of De Queen and sits along Hwy 71 on its way to Texarkana. Their team in years past had not been a strong team and De Queen usually won the games. This team, however, put up a strong effort against us for about three quarters of the game. I particularly remember playing an interior defensive lineman position and being faced with repeated dive plays from large backfield players. I must have stopped or impeded those plays sufficiently to prevent the gains they desired from their offense.

Toward the start of the 4th Quarter, one of their linebackers tried to jump over our offensive center's back on the start of a play. He didn't make it and wound up kicking our player's helmet with his cleated shoe. The referees called a penalty on their defense and marked off 10 or 15 yards. That seemed to break the backs of their unit, and we went on to easily win the game. Later, in the dressing room, our head coach got up on a stool and told us: "You are the best "team" I have ever coached!"

Transportation from the school to home after games was always an issue, especially for "away games." I realized that the bus driver, Virgil, lived further out in the community from where I lived, and I could catch a ride with him on the bus as he drove it back to his house after those away games. He dropped me off in the middle of the night at the road junction where my brothers and I caught the school bus daily. I had to walk the half a mile plus distance in the middle of the night to get home. This was a little scary as I passed along a wooded section on the way up the hill to come in front of the Turner's house, but I just steeled myself by thinking that there was nothing there at night that wasn't there during the day and walked on. My daddy's brothers and sisters used to love telling tales about panthers, some jumping out of trees during the night, but I didn't think about that. On some nights, however, there were glow worms laying on the surface of the road, which I investigated and dismissed as a cause for concern.

At one time near the end of the season, an assistant coach, who was also the basketball coach, was giving me and some others a ride home after practice in the old Ford school pickup. He said to me that he had been told that I had a daddy who was a "Son of a Bitch." That was obviously true, but I said nothing because what was I to say? Nothing I would have said would have made any difference.

Post Season

At the end of the season, we again, on Thanksgiving Day, played Texarkana, Arkansas High School, this time at their field. The day was sunny, but cool and somewhat hazy. The Texarkana team players were noticeably larger than ours and they played in a different conference that included bigger schools in Arkansas and some (probably) in Texas.

In the game they ran their plays and gained a lot of yardage, but they also incurred many penalties that negated a lot of those gains. They scored only one touchdown, which speaks well for our defense against this larger team. Our team persisted in our efforts in both offense and defense and our offense was driving toward their goal line toward the end of the game. The final play was a pass from our quarterback to an "end" player near the goal line. The pass was low, almost caught, but ultimately dropped, thus ending the game. I learned later that the Texarkana fans were very worried about how close we were to scoring and tying up the game.

We had a good and winning season, and I received some recognition and awards for my play. I was selected to be "All-District" for my position and I received the "Most Outstanding Player" award from a local civic club. The day the award was handed out, the team was invited for lunch in the local café where the civic club had their meetings. I had no idea the award was going to be handed out and didn't even know about the luncheon until I arrived at school. I was wearing my "White Cords" (corduroy) pants, which were fashionable in Oregon, and a gold shirt: hardly style of dressing I would have chosen, had I known the award luncheon was coming.

After I was named as the winner, I stood up, accepted the trophy, and simply said, "I'm honored to be the recipient of this award." I took the trophy home and showed it to my mother. She was pleased, although she really gave me no reaction. Years later, when there was a recounting of past award winners in the newspaper: "The De Queen Bee," she told me that she had been asked by a friend if that was her son? She said was pleased to say "Yes!" Although this was about fifty years late, it still felt good to have the pride of a parent voiced.

After receiving the award, I was interviewed by a reporter for the Dierks Forests Incorporated company newspaper: the company where my daddy was employed. A write-up appeared in that newspaper, which, incidentally, omitted the part about my being in the Glee Club choir. I can understand why that omission occurred, and that was okay with me. In all of this, however, there was never any word of recognition, and certainly not any approval from my daddy. As stated earlier, he, if anything, acted like he was insulted. There are bound to have been working companions of his who would have commented on this to him, and I wonder how he received those congratulatory comments. As I also stated earlier, about the time this all happened, he had come up with his edict, out of the blue, that I could not use the family car.

Basketball

I always enjoyed basketball; maybe that was because it is played at night and the gyms were always filled with lights and people close by in the stands and there was an electricity feeling to it all. There was also the satisfaction, whether individually or because of a team effort, of making a score in the game and sometimes that occurred several times during the games. I also developed a jump shot that I was quite proficient at it, putting the ball in the basket from longer ranges on the court. The coach commented on me doing something I was not aware of: he said I was putting the ball behind my head as I prepared to release the ball. That was just a natural move for me, and it certainly helped me align the ball with the arc to the goal.

About a month before the end of the season, the coach kicked four of the "star" players off the team. I don't know what happened, or why the action was taken, but I suspect it had a lot to do with the "Big Stud" attitude of those players, who had been frontline players through their years in junior high and high school. As a result, however, I got to be one of the starters and was moved from being a "Forward" to being a "Guard" doing a lot of ball handling in the forecourt and starting the offensive plays and maneuverings that would position the team for scoring.

In one game with a nearby town's high school team, the coach told to team in a court side time out to "Feed Cap, he's hot!" I scored at least 14 points in that game, and afterward I wasn't hesitant about taking a shot when an opening appeared. In a game against Mena, in our gym, I took a couple of long-range shots, at the three-point range today, and made both, with the ball swishing through the net without hitting the rim at all. The crowd let out huge cheers when both shots sank through the basket.

At another time, after the halftime break, when the starting "Jump Ball" was tossed, I took control of the tipped ball and started a body motion toward the goal we had played on offense during the half. After the first half, the goals are switched so we played offense on the opposite end of the court. With my motion both teams ran to that end of the court. I recognized the mistake and dribbled the ball down, unopposed, down to our new goal and made an easy lay-up for the score. The crowd broke out in laughter at the event.

We also played our archrival high school team from Nashville and had a difficult time with them. They were very adept at faking "charging" violations against the opposing teams. They literally would fold a leg behind themselves and fall to the floor without even being touched by an opposing player. This resulted in a lot of "charging" fouls being charged on the offensive player, when none had occurred. We played them in the district championship tournament, and they pulled the same tactic on me when I made a feint move toward one player and probably came no closer to him than a foot and a half away. He fell to the floor in his faked fashion, and I was called for a foul. Apparently, one referee noticed the fake play and told the other referee about it, because the next time that fake play was made, the referee called the foul on that defensive player.

Track

In the spring of that year, track season followed basketball; I, of course, ran on the track team and was a "quarter miler" and a high jumper. I wasn't particularly fast when running and I wasn't that good of a jumper, but I was better than a lot of others and I was a determined runner. Coach told me "Your try as hard as anybody out there, but you're just not that fast." I was good enough to run in the mile relay, however, and I ran the first leg or the second leg in several races.

In one Quarter Mile race in Nashville, where they had a cinder surfaced track, the marked off lanes were "staggered" for equal distances to the finish line. I was assigned to the outermost lane. That one has the biggest stagger, and the starting point is several yards in front of the next inside lane. The other lanes had similar staggers progressively back to the first lane being on the Start/Finish line. I started off leading the pack, but after rounding the first turn, the others were catching up with me and, of course, passed me as I rounded the second turn and ran toward the finish line. I may have been last to finish, or next-to-last, but it didn't matter as I had given it my best.

I must include the story of two members of the team who decided to compete in the pole-vaulting event at one of these track meets. Apparently, they had not practiced this event prior to this meet and were just out giving it their best effort. Turns out they were the winners of the event. Years later at a class reunion they said they had cleared 10 Ft. with their winning efforts. At the next track meet, however, it was a much different story; they said they "forgot" how they had vaulted previously and couldn't compete.

Senior Academic Year

Chemistry (not my favorite), Physics (I really enjoyed this subject, because it explained how things worked), Trigonometry (juxta positioning the parts of a triangle didn't resonate with me), Solid Geometry (very interesting, actually), and a self-taught typing class was my curriculum, along with the sports teams and Glee Club, was enough to keep me busy (and beyond) during this year.

As I mentioned earlier, I was also elected Senior Class President, but it happened without it being a sought-out position. A class meeting was called with all 66 members of the class present. The senior English teacher, who was an excellent teacher, called me to the front and instructed me to conduct the election. I thought, "Okay, I can do that" and proceeded to call for nominations. I was one of those nominated, and was, subsequently, elected President, by the class.

Later, some members of the class made the comment that anyone placed in the position of conducting the election would have been elected, and that very well could have been true, but the class sponsor English teacher and other faculty members thought well of me and there were many in the class who, obviously, respected me as well. The English teacher had, earlier, told me privately that I was a "Very easy person to look at," and I took that as encouragement to help improve my self-image. I had been in a Speech Class of Her's in the previous year and was part of the cast of a Halloween play presented to the public: "Mystery in the library." I can't see how the audience would have been very well entertained by our very amateur acting; let's just say it was a growth experience for us students.

I don't know that any of this was reflected in life in my home; I had no reason to mention my activities with my parents and certainly didn't want any interaction with my daddy if I could avoid it. None the less, it was about mid-October that he came up with the edict that I could no longer use the family car. That was without any conflict with him, and certainly very little contact.

Activities

Due to being class president, I was part of the Student Council. A friend of mine, "Henry," was the president of the council and all classes in the school had representatives. Henry had run for the president position the previous spring and was elected; I had run for vice president, and was not elected, which turned out better for me in the long run. I did pick up the additional duty of raising the school's American Flag in the mornings. I didn't do very well at that because I tried to do it all myself, and between catching the school bus and being late for Glee club practice, and then trying to raise the flag before class, the flag didn't get raised in a timely fashion. I realize now that having the responsibility, and doing the work, are two different things: what I should have done (no one suggested this) was to ask for volunteers and work with them as a manager to ensure that the flag raising got accomplished.

Henry's mother, who was a teacher I had previously for a couple of classes in junior high, took an unusual interest in me and invited me into her home occasionally, the first of which was for an afternoon coffee. I took the coffee, added some sugar to it and thought it was pretty good. I invited Henry to go squirrel hunting with me and he did, but he did not bring a gun because he didn't have a license. I didn't have a license either, but I don't think it would have been required because I was seventeen at the time. We didn't see any squirrels, which was just as well with me.

It was a busy year, much of it was memorable for me, and I had good, positive experiences. There was a school talent show that was arranged and held during the spring. Somehow, it was decreed that I should be the master of ceremonies, and that I should dress up as a cowboy pantomiming to playing of the Rawhide theme music from the TV show to start the show. I didn't have any "cowboy" attire, so one of the teachers loaned me one of her husband's shirts to wear during the performance. So, there I was, with a leather bull whip in hand, pretending to be Rowdy Yates From "Rawhide" to start the show.

I was also the M.C. introducing all the acts; to fill the gap between the acts I came up with a series of jokes that I found in Boy's Life Magazine in the school library. One of them I adapted was about the science teacher and the math teacher who were fishing companions outside of school. It was about them going fishing in a swamp-like area of the county called "Pond Creek Bottom," where they were set upon by two very large mosquitos. One mosquito was reported to have said to the other, "Shall we eat them here, or take them back into the swap? The other mosquito responded: "Let's eat them here, if we take them back into the swamp, the big ones will take them away from us!" It was fun, people enjoyed the show, and I was told I did a very good job.

The school year was a busy time, with all the classwork (and homework), athletics Homecoming ritual, school carnival, concession stand support, SAT testing, Christmas decoration (Henry and I cut a cedar tree from a neighbor's property and erected it on campus – it was a lot heavier that I had anticipated), class administration and choir activities. Toward the end of the year, I had so much work to do out of class that I had to start neglecting some of it so I could accomplish other projects. I managed to do enough in all classes to pass but made a final grading period "F" in a math class, although I passed the course. Today, I still wonder if all of that was necessary.

In the Spring, the choir (Glee Club) made a trip to Hot Springs for the yearly competition of choirs. I'm not sure how we did in the competition, but, prior to the trip, a few athletes had joined the Glee Club when they learned that trips would be taken by the choir later in the year. The club music teacher wasn't really pleased with the new members and asked me privately how they were doing with practicing the music. I told her that one of the members had been counting time intervals with his hand, when "rests" were in the music score, and was making efforts to learn the music. That seemed to satisfy her, and the new members remained.

With these new members some athletic team practices were introduced to the club. The football team had a sign above the dressing room exit that read "Come back a winner." When exiting the room, each player would slap the sign with one hand. At this choir competition one of those players/choir members told the group to hit an imaginary sign as they exited the room. We all did that and that was a good thing, I believe.

One of the choir members had some relatives in Hot Springs, one of whom was a junior girl student at the school. She had a new '58 Chevy Impala convertible and I was invited, along with some others, to come along as she took it for a drive. I remember some pedestrians on the sidewalk waving to us and I never thought to wave back, it just wasn't in my experience to do so.

Later, a few of us went to dinner at the "Vapors" night club. This was back in the time when gambling was still possible in Hot Springs and the "Vapors' was a swanky place. I don't remember what I chose, but Henry had a Chef Salad with an anchovy on top, I had never seen that before.

A dance at the school followed and we all attended. A girl trio sang "Harbor Lights," which was a popular song at the time, and it sounded wonderful to me. I thought it could have been that these girls were part of the entertainment scene for the clubs in Hot Springs, which easily could have been true. The member's girl cousin was with us at the dance and another fellow and I were with her. I told her she had two escorts for the dance, but, as it turns out, I was the one she liked.

She and I later exchanged letters, and she invited me to visit her in her home, which I did toward the end of the school year. Her mother served us filet mignon, which I had never had before. There was a wooden toothpick holding the bacon on the sides and, I guess, I ate it, because it wasn't removed, or was never there originally. There were no bad aftereffects, however.

I visited her again upon my return from Oregon at the end of the summer, but the relationship never progressed from that point.

Oregon III

My third summer in Oregon was, again, a pleasure for me, but this time a school classmate of mine, Billy, who was also a football player, accompanied me on the bus ride across the western U.S. This was his first time traveling away from home and just before leaving the bus station in De Queen, his mother privately asked me to look out for him on the trip. We did fine, but Billy smoked cigarettes at times, and one time in Salt Lake City I believe, I smoked a cigarette with him while we were outside the bus. It left me feeling "jumpy" and I didn't repeat that on the trip or later.

He had relatives in Salem and stayed with them during the summer, but that family at times came to where I was and worked in the fields. When David, the farmer I worked for, found out about Billy, he made the comment that, if he had known about Billy earlier, he could have made a place in the barn for him to stay; that didn't sound like pleasant accommodations to me; luckily, nothing was forthcoming from that comment. I drove up to Salem a few times to visit him during the summer and once late in the summer, after a phone call from Billy, I felt I needed to go visit him for moral support I guess, and we drove over to the Oregon Coast that afternoon. We visited Depot Bay, which I had visited with my family back in '55 on the first trip out there. The scenery was beautiful, and it was a very enjoyable trip. I remember stopping at a local café and having Miller beer; It was the "Champagne of bottled beer," per the advertising at the time. I was not asked for any proof of age for my purchase of it with my meal and I never gave that a second thought.

The softball team had a new sponsor, the Stoddard-Frink Chevrolet Co., and one of the owners, Bob, was a former player and an experienced pitcher with a unique "Rise ball." That means that the backward-spinning ball, instead of sinking on its way to the plate, would rise from the original flight path; obviously, it was difficult for the batters to hit those pitches. For the first time, the team had uniforms, dark blur with white piping on the seams and the sponsor's name on them as well.

At one of the games, two young women appeared at the field and, from all indications, were looking for "companionship," at least for a while it seems. Events transpired that these two young ladies drew the attention of two young men on the team. One of those was my ride to the games. After the game, these two young ladies and the young men, I made a third, got together and somehow decided to go swimming at night in the swiftly flowing water of the Santiam River at a low water crossing that the young men knew about, maybe the girls too, I don't know. I went along and we stopped at my house to get my swim trunks. We changed into swimsuits in the darkness along the riverbank and into the water we went, plunging off the concrete roadway of the crossing.

Afterward, we changed back into our clothing and left the river. I could see what was going on and I was the odd man out in that situation and told my friend to drop me off at my grandmother's house, which he did. The next day at my friend's house, his mother tried to pump me for information on what had happened. It seems my friend came home without his shirt, and she was trying to find out what had gone on. I kept mum though she tried various stratagems to get me to talk. She said, at one point, "He knows what happened," but I didn't say anything... I, thankfully, never heard anything further about this.

My Car

Shortly after I arrived that summer and returned to work for David, he told me he was going to get me a car to use as transportation between the various farm fields during the days and I would have the car to use otherwise on nights and weekends. We would split the cost for the purchase of the car between us. We looked around the used car lots of Albany and found two candidates: one was a Ford, and the other was an unusual Plymouth business coupe, both priced at about $100. The Plymouth Couple was the cheaper one, at $90, but we were told it had been used by the electrical power company and had an overhauled engine, plus it had a through windshield post spotlight- that worked. We agreed on the Plymouth coupe and bought it.

I had to make it a bit more stylish and current with hot rods on the west coast as best I could, so I took the hubcaps off, painted the wheels black and got some fake "whitewalls" for the tires. The car had a bit of a "rake" front end, so that made it fit in better with the local hotrodders.

Speaking of "Hotrodders," there was a local young guy who worked sometimes in the fields, he drove a '39 Chevrolet sedan that had been painted a candied green color and had "chrome reverse" wheels rims for the tires; it was a sharp-looking car. He told me that he had at one time put some model airplane fuel into its gas tank and had outrun a new Chevy that had a V-8 engine. which was one of the newer models at that time.

After the softball games, we did a lot of cruising the drive-ins around Albany, a nice local one was the "Tom -Tom" located out near the interstate highway. On the streets between the drive-ins, there was an often-seen '55 Chevy with the name "Tiny Tub" painted on it. On another occasion there was a '30's something coupe with a dragon painted on the rear trunk lid. Supposedly it was owned by a highly reputed artist from Los Angeles.

At the end of the summer, David told me I could have his interest in the car, and I could call it a bonus, or whatever. That gave me, and my friend Billy, a way to return to Arkansas. I was just reaching my 18th birthday at that time.

In preparation for the trip, I bought two new front tires, and had a neighbor, who was an auto mechanic, do a tune-up on the engine. I also replaced the oil-bath air cleaner with a paper, universal fit, one. These preparations worked out well for the trip.

The first day, I drove to Salem to pick up Billy, then we stopped for breakfast in a local café. There was some discussion of our trip with the people in the café and they wished us good luck as we prepared to leave. We left and headed east into the Cascade Mountains. After climbing through them, we were upon the high desert of central Oregon and drove on to a town in Idaho where my older brother was visiting his girlfriend whom he had met in college and who had accompanied him to my grandmother's home the week earlier.

My buddy and I spent the night with her family then headed out the next day into Utah, and Salt Lake City, into southern Colorado and on into and across New Mexico. We stopped for the night at a motel in State Line, New Mexico, then headed out the next morning into and across the Panhandle region of Texas. We left Texas and entered Oklahoma at Vernon, where we picked up Hwy. 70 heading toward Arkansas.

We stopped at a drive-in barbeque restaurant in Ardmore for lunch. When we looked at the menu painted on the side of the building, we noticed an item that was listed as "Doc's Favorite Pig." Someone had scratched in beside it "The Carhop," meaning the waitress. I thought that was funny and I still get a chuckle remembering that today.

We arrived in mid-afternoon and pulled to a stop in the circular drive under the trees at my parent's home. My mother came running out to greet us. I'm sure she was vastly relieved we had made the trip safely. That car was a good one and I drove it for about two and a half years before I went into the Air Force.

CHAPTER NINE
COLLEGE AND BEYOND

.

While I was in Oregon, I registered at the University of Arkansas, Fayetteville to begin my studies to become an engineer. I had sent in my $10 registration fee for the dorm room, but I really had no idea how I was going to pay for college. All of that would change when I visited a friend and found out he was going to Texarkana Junior College and his mother urged me to do the same. This turned out to be the best choice I could have made.

I filled out the application forms and was accepted. My friend and I then visited with the head football coach. I told him about my experiences and honors gained while playing with the Leopards in De Queen High School. He listened and thought I could fit in at the tight end position on his team. As a result, I moved into the athletic dorm at the college in advance of the school year and began practicing with the team.

My dorm roommate was the team quarterback, who seemed rather short and small to me, but he was very muscular and must have been an excellent athlete to be in his position. The dorm mother (administrator) had asked me, when interviewed with her before moving in "Are you a Christian?" I felt uncomfortable about being asked that, but I answered, considering all the indoctrination I had earlier in life, and the mandatory church attendance and home practices, that the answer was "Yes." I assume she placed me in the same room as the quarterback because had his Bible in the room and was a mild-mannered person, unlike many of the other players in the dorm.

The players were, seemingly much larger than the ones I had played with, and against before in high school and I practiced with the offensive line, part of that was pushing sleds with two other larger guys and I had trouble keeping my end of the sled advancing at the same rate as the other guys were doing. We never got to the point of practicing as an entire offensive unit, and I never practiced at catching any passes. I do remember that the calisthenics being less intensive than I had known previously and my muscles became very sore very quickly after practice started.

My stint with the football team didn't last long; I had signed on hoping to get a scholarship. After a week, I was told that it wasn't forthcoming, but they would like me to stay on the team. Thinking about that later, I realized there, most probably, was never any possibility of a scholarship initially because they didn't have one to offer. I don't have any animosity regarding that situation, however, as it was a good experience and, had my financial situation been different, I may have stayed on the team. I had signed up for 19 hours of classes, and I felt it best not to continue if no financial assistant was part of the equation. Maybe that was not the best decision, but, as it worked out, I would not have been able to accept another forthcoming opportunity when it arose later that semester.

I used my savings from working in Oregon to pay for my college expenses and I needed to extend that as much as possible. About mid-term an opportunity came up with the Red River Army Depot, which was located about 10 miles to the west of Texarkana, to be an Engineering Aide on a six-month program working half-days during the week. This was a godsend for me, and I quickly made an application and was accepted into the program. There were about eight of us in the program, one of those joined the Air Force with me a couple of years later.

The engineering aide experience was a good one and I did well; the job was mostly tracking conveyor systems changes in the various buildings and doing some engineering drawings. The main task I accomplished was creating an ink-on-linen enlarged layout of a computer punch-card. That was a tedious task requiring very careful management of the ink lettering devices and the ink to fill them. More than once, I had to carefully remove a drop of ink from the linen surface. I did this with the very sharp blade of a small pocketknife by slicing under the ink drop after it had dried.

The Barbershop Incident

I got word that a barber, who had been working in De Queen, had moved to Texarkana, and was working in a barbershop in a downtown hotel located near the train station. Out of a sense of loyalty to a former local, I went there one afternoon in the spring for a haircut. As I sat and waited my turn in the chair, an older gentleman walked into the shop, looked around and said, "Let's have some fun at this man's expense," while pointing at me.

I was, of course, very wary about this and wondered what he was going to do. He started by passing his hand around my head without touching me. After doing so, he said "This man is almost a genius at mathematics, the vibrations are that strong." He made some other comments about some of my relationships with girls, but said my wife's name would start with an "E." That has not been the case except my first girlfriend's name was Elaine, and we know what happened there.

He then passed his hand along and around my body; he stopped on my left side just below the ribcage and asked, "What's going on here?' in that area I have had, then and over the years, some mild pain and discomfort in the area. I think this has to do with the spleen, but nothing further has come of it. He next passed his hand over the inside of my left thigh and asked, "What's here?" That was where I got a scar from the pre-school incident with the jagged wheel rim. He then asked about the inside of my left foot where I have another scar.

It then became time for me to have my hair cut and I went and sat down in the barber's chair. When I was settled, he came up and said, "Now I'm going to hypnotize you." I thought to myself "There's no way I'm going to let that happen, but he was persistent and, as he continued his efforts, I lowered my chin down to my chest. I think that was to avoid having to look at him, but I don't know that for sure. He finally gave up and said, "You're fighting like a pig, but It could be done; it would take about 30 minutes."

I did go back to that barbershop afterward, but that man never appeared again when I was there.

The UFO Visitation

I must preface this story with the disclaimer that this is entirely hearsay from some friends of mine, but, hopefully, this is interesting, nonetheless.

Two friends of mine and co-students at the college: Ronald and Eddie, were riding with me one Sunday night as I drove back to Texarkana College. On the way we talked, and the conversation got around to UFO's. Ronald told about being out in a wooded area at night and watching an object move around the sky. Eddie then told of a friend who had a dream that beings had entered his home, got him out of bed, took him outside and took him inside a craft sitting there in his side yard. The beings explained the workings of the craft then took him back inside his home.

The next morning, when this person exited his home, outside there had been a heavy dew during the night that left the grass glistening in the sunlight but, in a spot where the craft had been, was a dewless depression and the was evidence of footprints leading to and from that depression.

Summer Work

I got a construction job with Dierks Forests Inc. after the school semester ended to help build an expansion to the fiber board manufacturing facility at a place called "Craig" across the state line over in Oklahoma. It was west of the Mountain Fork River and south of Hwy 70. Later I was transferred to work on the start of a gypsum drywall board manufacturing facility northwest of Nashville, Arkansas at a place called "Briar." When interviewed by the construction superintendent, who was stated to be a full-blooded native American, he commented that I was, "An 18-year-old, right out of high school." I didn't correct him and tell him about my college engineering student status and my work as an engineering aide, but that got to be known later.

Before I could take the job, I had to overhaul the engine of my 49 Plymouth, which had developed some problems. Those included a leaking valve and some cracked piston rings which were caused by overheating (I've learned that a faulty water distribution tube was the cause of that). I did most of the work myself, which included all the disassembly and reassembly of the engine. The valves were ground by a local garage and the garage owner's son, who was in my class, helped with reassembly of the piston bearings and connection of the connecting rods to the crankshaft. After completing the work, the engine started and ran well without any problems for all the time I used the car. I must add that, after the work was completed and the car was started, my daddy seemed pleased and made a comment that if this one didn't use oil, he would be happy. To be fair, I must add that he helped me tow the car to and from the garage for the valve work. He had also helped me to solve a gas starvation problem earlier.

Two other young men from my high school but were a class behind me and had just graduated that year, got construction jobs with Dierks. We often shared driving to work responsibilities, and we worked a lot of the time together. On one occasion at the Briar site, the superintendent was visiting there and saw a job that needed to be done to speed up an on-going operation setting up building support poles and cementing them into the ground. The poles had to be set exactly on pre-determined spots. He hollered at me, called me by my name, and instructed me and my two friends/working companions to come and take over an operation that was determining and marking those center points. We did that by stretching long wires from horizontal length and width markings on building outline boards erected all around the planned new building. Where the wires crossed was the center points for the pole locations. I think the superintendent had found out about my engineering training and experience.

An Excursion to the Lake

A high school friend and I decided that, on a Sunday in early June, we would drive over to lake Greeson, which was about a seventy-mile drive northeast from De Queen. It lies in the Ouachita Mountains in the vicinity of the Albert Pike area, but downriver from there. The lake was formed years previously by the creation of a Corps of Engineers dam at a narrow passage of the river near Murfreesboro, Ar. It was called Narrows Lake for a long time before the name was changed to Lake Greeson. The area is quite nice with rocky shorelines and clear clean waters. After arriving there and looking around, we decided to drive on up to Hot Springs, which was less than fifty miles and drop in on the girl I had met there, and in whose home, I had spent the previous weekend.

We arrived in Hot Springs and found she was at a youth service at her church, we found her car at the church and waited for the service to end. After visiting her for a short while in her home, we headed out, and on the way, we came to a junction on the highway that, if taken, would lead us to Hope, Ar. where the girlfriend of my friend lived. We decided to take the drive to Hope and see if he could get in touch with her. It was getting a little late when we arrived in Hope and found her house. There was no response when my friend rang her doorbell, so we headed back toward De Queen which took us through Nashville.

Nashville, again, was the archrival of De Queen in high school sports. After my friend and I passed through the town and west past the edge of town, we came to the top of a small rise in the road, after which the highway dropped down to a narrow iron bridge crossing a small river. On the bridge were two cars, facing opposite directions, stopped on the bridge taking up both lanes. I slowed to a stop on the hill and waited for the cars to move on.

After they moved apart, I eased up and then passed the car which had been facing the same direction I had been traveling. As we passed, the two young guys in the car saw that we were two young guys as well and then began chasing us. Their car was a recent model Ford with a V-8 engine, and I was driving my '49 Plymouth. I floored my gas pedal and drove as fast as it would take us. I was slower, but I had the lead, and I wasn't going to allow them to pass me. They tried several times, but I blocked their move and kept ahead of them. This went on for about 10 miles until the other driver finally gave up and dropped off my rear. We traveled the rest of the way without incident. Not sure what would have happened, had they passed us, but it could have been a fight there on the road.

When I entered the house after arriving home, my mother met me and asked if we had been to Hot Springs. I said "Yes," and she said she had thought that's what we had done.

Next College Year

I worked the rest of the summer and returned to college classes in the fall, but I lived at home and mostly rode the school bus that ran from our town to the college daily. On some days I drove my car and if another student wanted to ride, I would agree if they bought the gas. It cost $2.00 worth of gas for a round trip.

After working the construction job during the summer, I got a job at a gas station owned by my friend Ronald's father, working on weekends. I subsequently learned about a maintenance job at the local chicken processing plant where I could make much better wages, but I had to work from 6 AM to 6 PM on both Saturday and Sunday. The crew was run under the direction of the chief of maintenance for the processing plant, who was the father of one of my friends. He was in the class ahead of me in high school. That friend later went into the Air Force, became a fighter pilot, served in Viet Nam and after making the military his career, was promoted to" General."

The maintenance manager turned out to be a very "hands off" manager and most of the work we did was what we chose to do based on the directions of a team lead person. The first task for a group of us was cleaning and painting, with red lead paint, the rafters of the metal building roof. This was a tedious task and required that the rafters be scrapped of the rust spots and dirt that was on them before repainting. The first site chosen for this was over the pit where the chicken heads and internals were deposited in dump trucks prior to their transport to a rendering facility – as I understood.

The work at the site was completed and the crew moved into the main open area of the building which had very high roof structures. We would have to erect scaffolding three and four units high to reach the work areas and work from 2×12 boards that we mounted on the top of the scaffolding. Looking back, it was dangerous and dirty work with probable exposure to toxic chemicals. I kept that job working weekends into the spring of that year. A friend said I was looking very haggard at that time.

In the spring semester I sought out the college choir director and, after an extensive audition, was allowed to join the choir as a baritone. This was a good experience and a girl, who later became my wife, was in the choir also and, although we were just friends, did some paling around together with some other choir members that we both enjoyed. The choir did a lot of Latin cantata works, Broadway show tunes and other musical works. We did a version of Ave' Maria that had me soloing the very intricate introduction. At a concert we performed at a local high school, the choir, afterward, assembled in the base of a stone water tower and sang that work, noting the excellent acoustics that were generated. We also took a two-week tour of south Texas performing in schools and churches. It was an enjoyable and worthwhile experience.

Upon returning from the trip, I did not report back to the chicken processing plant work crew. That was a mistake, as

I started having to borrow money weekly for daily college expenses. He gave me $5.00 for the week each time I asked, and it was money I knew I would have to repay.

The Ice Storm

During the winter months, late January or February, an Ice storm arrived one school day during the afternoon hours. I had driven my '49 Plymouth to the college that day, so, not having a place to spend the night, I prepared to drive back home on the ice.

The trip on Hwy 71 went reasonably well until I crossed the Little River Bridge. The roadway after the bridge was elevated with steep embankments on both sides with narrow shoulders. I was following some traffic in front of me when there was some slowing and I had to react quickly to slow the car. As I was slowing there was some loss of traction, and I entered a skid toward the narrow road shoulder. After some wiggling movement, I managed, somehow, to regain control and stay on the roadway.

About a mile and a half, to two miles, from the river bridge the road makes a turn to the west and a half mile later begins an ascent up the face of a mountain to a hilly plateau. A line of cars was stopped at the bottom of the hill-climbing stretch of highway. I waited until my turn came to begin the ascent.

At first, I drove while keeping the car on the hard surfaced roadway but found the going to be very slippery. I soon realized that I could possibly get better traction and directional control by running with my right wheels on the gravel coated shoulder and that's what I did. After several more minutes I was at the top and feeling confident I could complete my journey.

Several miles later, as the road started to approach Lockesburg, I topped the last rise of the roadway and, consequently, lost the additional traction provided by the uphill gravity effects on the car. I went into a spin and wound up across the opposite lane with my rear wheels on the shoulder and the engine stalled. Luckily no on-coming traffic was present at the time. I restarted the engine and, with the rear wheels on the gravel of the shoulder, was able to pull the car back on the roadway and proceed on my way; however, much more slowly and carefully this time.

I made it home with no additional problems and counted myself lucky to do so. The next day I borrowed the family's Ford pickup, put some additional weight in the bed to improve traction and made the trips down and back without incident.

The Last Summer in Oregon

I had no known prospects for employment near home, so I investigated going, once again, to Oregon. I called my grandmother and got her concurrence to live with her and Cecil. I called David and got his concurrence for a job, so I borrowed my bus fare from my parents, boarded the bus and headed west.

I don't remember anything definite about the bus ride, but I do remember arriving in Albany in the middle of the night. I didn't want to sleep in the bus station, and I knew there was a hotel a few blocks down the street, so I picked up my bags and walked there. When I entered the lobby there was no one in sight. Then I heard a voice from the open balcony on the 2nd floor, which ringed the entire lobby, that said "What do you want?" I said, "I'd like a room." The night person appeared and signed me in for a $4.00 room.

That room had a bed and a toilet and that was about it, but it was entirely sufficient for my needs. The next morning, I called my grandmother and later they came into town and picked me up.

I went to talk with David, and he volunteered his opinion that I could easily find employment at higher wages than he could pay. We found a 1953 Chevrolet that seemed suitable, and was less than $200, and he bought it for me.

I was almost immediately contacted by the son of a community family who were friends with my grandmother and Cecil, whose name, incidentally, was also "Jerry." He told me that Edwards Sawmill in Albany was starting up a second shift. This was the "swing" shift that worked from 3:00 in the afternoon to midnight. I applied for the job, was hired, and placed beside Jerry on the sawed lumber conveyor to grade and separate the newly sawn boards from log core pieces that needed to be sawed into smaller boards in an operation called "Resaw."

Jerry would mark the pieces, and I would operate a foot lever that raised some forks allowing the resaw pieces to drop onto a conveyor running over to the resaw operation. I found I couldn't just let the log pieces fall onto the conveyor, but rather had to try to position them so that the far end was on the opposite side of the conveyor. I did this by applying pressure on the end of the log, pulling it toward me as it fell. This was all I could do, be it seemed to work well enough.

Next to me, on my left, was a multiple-ganged saw that cut off the ends of the boards to make them standard lengths. It had a whirling row of about two-foot diameter saws that, when selected by the operator, would drop down and quickly saw through the board that was in position. The operator had a small lever for each saw and would flip them down as needed. The lumber was flowing along the conveyor up to the saws quite rapidly and that operator had to be very quick of mind and hand. Not surprisingly, that employee was a young man, maybe a little older than me, who was very agile and appeared to think very rapidly.

One afternoon, as I was driving on the road leading to the mill, there was a young policeman stopping traffic. He saw me and my lunch and surmised that I was a worker reporting for the 2nd shift. He informed me there was a fire in the drying kiln and that I probably would be fighting the fire when I got to the mill. That turned out to be true and I manned the fire hose for that shift. The next night the mill was back to normal operation, for the processing of green lumber, that is.

The night when I told the foreman I would be leaving the next day to return to college, he said he wanted to bring a new guy into that position and wanted to break him in as soon as possible (I don't think that should really take very long). He told me to go out and work on the mill pond positioning the floating logs to be picked up by a conveyor chain to take them into the primary saw operation.

The area was lit by some lights and by a fire burning in a teepee-like containing device. The scrap from the mill was being burned in that device.

On the pond that night I was walking on floating logs and using a long pike to move the logs into position to go up the conveyor and, of course, I fell off one of the logs into the water. I scrambled out of the water, then took off my wet shirt and hung it on a bush near the trash burner to try to dry it out. Later, I found that the drying strategy had worked well and put my shirt back on. After arriving home that night, I took a shower in the unheated water available for the shower, to rid myself of whatever I may have been exposed to in the inky black water of that mill pond.

End of Summer and Return

I sold my '53 Chevy for $150, after taking out an ad in the Albany paper, so I recouped part of my investment there.

There was an older couple, who were friends with my grandmother, and, coincidentally, planning a trip to visit relatives in Missouri at the time I needed to return to start the fall semester in school. They had a '58 Chevy to drive on the trip and were looking for some help in doing the driving. They wanted me to go along, do some of the driving and share in the cost of gas. That was okay with me, as it would certainly be a lot less costly than other transportation.

The plan was that we would leave in the afternoon, drive all night and the next day, then stop somewhere and spend the night before resuming the drive. A second night in transit was not planned.

We started out and drove through the Cascade Mountains, then out on the high desert of eastern Oregon. About sundown as I was driving, I noticed that the engine temperature gauge was over, all the way, into the extremely hot range. I pulled over to the side of the road and we opened the hood; the engine was so hot that oil on the outside of the engine was bubbling –this was definitely not a good sign.

As luck would have it, it wasn't long before an older flatbed truck pulled into a stop behind us. The driver was a fellow that could have best been described as an "Okie." That was fine with us, and, thinking back over the event, he seemed like an angel sent at the right time. He had the tools needed and he helped us pull out the engine thermostat that was frozen shut, thus shutting off the flow of engine coolant to the radiator. We reattached the thermostat housing, added the water we had to the radiator and drove on into the next town. We stopped at a service station where the owner had the engine oil changed; that may, or may not, have been necessary, but I thought it was certainly a good idea.

We drove on through the rest of the night and made our way through Idaho and into Wyoming. That afternoon, I noticed the older man nodding off while he was driving. I then volunteered to take over the driving that day until we decided to stop at a motel we found for the night. I got a separate room and slept until the gentleman banged on my door the next morning.

I drove a lot that second day and remember especially driving into Denver and slowing the car, thinking we would soon be on city streets, but then I realized that the multilane highway was not quickly turning into speed restricted city streets, and I sped it up to the appropriate speeds.

We soon turned off that highway at the city center, went by the state capitol building and picked up Hwy 287, which runs all the way from Texas to Denver. I was destined to travel that road many times in the coming years.

It was then off onto the high plains of eastern Colorado and driving at the higher speeds that seemed appropriate for thinly populated regions. We made it into Kansas and drove on until we reached Nevada, Missouri about midnight. This was the place where I could catch a ride on the bus line that ran from Kansas City to De Queen.

It wasn't long before a bus came by, and I got on. When I walked down the aisle looking for a seat, there was one, on the aisle, with a young lady sitting in the adjacent seat by the window. She said, "Can't you find a seat somewhere else?" I said, "I know just how you feel," but I took the seat anyway.

During the night we engaged in some chatter and found out we, strangely, had a lot in common: she had visited Piney Grove Bible Camp in De Queen when returning from the Bible Memory Association's Miracle Camp in Louisiana and we talked a lot about religious concepts during the night. So much so, that I became uncomfortable with the conversation and distanced myself during stops. She wrote a letter later and sent it to my home. My mother opened that letter before I got home that day, which I didn't like, of course, but there was nothing to be concerned about in the content. She said that she had told others about our coincidental meeting, and they marveled at the synchronicity of it all. It was, in reality, an amazing occurrence, but nothing further became of that relationship.

Return to School and Beyond.

I returned to Texarkana College, but for various reasons did not continue with the choir, although I wish I had. I signed up for a new class in Spanish that was, really, best suited and meant, I think, for those who already spoke Spanish and were looking for semester hour credits in that language. Many people, most of the class, dropped out and I tried to do that several times, but the college counselor kept me from it during that first half semester. I realized later that he did that to preserve the number of students in the class. At the start of the next half-semester I, again, asked to drop the course. The dean accepted my request and made comments that something was wrong with that class that caused so many people to drop out.

The effect that the counselor's denials of my requests during the first half semester was that a drop at that time would not have affected my Grade Point Average (GPA), but a drop after the start of the second half did affect my GPA, and it was a four-hour course. That GPA would later affect my application a couple of years later for an Air Force program that would have sent me through the rest of college for a bachelor's degree and earned me an officer's commission. In the end, however, I determined that an Air Force career was not what I was suited for, so maybe all of this was a blessing in disguise.

During the early weeks after the return to classes, some of my dormmates began talking about renting an apartment and living off campus. I was included in those discussions (why did people always come to me when they wanted to do something) and we rented an apartment across the street in a new complex just recently constructed. This was basically a good experience and provided a lot of socialization that might not have been available otherwise.

On Halloween, the apartment managers organized a Halloween party and, somehow, I got involved in helping secure the beverages. I had my car, so another fellow and I drove to his hometown of Foulk, Arkansas (famous for "The Foulk Monster") where we met up with a friend of his who was a "moonshiner, "i.e., a producer of untaxed illegal alcohol.

My friend talked with the young man who wanted to know about me and was I not an informant for the police, which my friend assured him I was not. Curiously, there was some talk I heard in later years that my friend may have, himself, been an undercover agent for the FBI. We then arranged to meet out on a country road where the delivery of the moonshine would occur. We drove out that road and, around a bend, we met we the friend and took delivery of two gallons of "White Lightening." We stashed that in the trunk of my car in an area in front of the rear axle where it would ride safely and drove back (across the state line) to the apartments.

When we arrived, we took the two gallons, which were in old Coca Cola gallon jugs, into the manager's apartment, where an older resident poured some of it into the open lid of one of the jugs and set it on fire. The alcohol burned with such a pale and clear blue flame that we had to turn off the lights before we could see it. It was definitely high proof alcohol.

The white lightning was mixed in a five to one ratio with fruit juices and placed in an old iron kettle that, at some time previously, could have been someone's wash pot. Dry ice was then added to the mix and that made a mixture that foamed and bubbled, much like a witch's brew.

At the party, people were drinking the mix like the fruit juice it tasted like, but after the second serving, they started to feel the alcohol, started having trouble talking and otherwise were exhibiting its effects. No one was hurt in any way by all of this, however, which was a good, if accidental, outcome.

Reckoning With Destiny

At the end of the semester, I had run out of money and could not continue with college, so, in order to avoid being drafted into the army, I enlisted in the Air Force, as did a friend of mine from college, who had been a part of the engineering aid program at Red River Army Depot. We enlisted on a "Buddy" plan and were in the same training "Flight," and assigned, later, to the same training school at Lowery Air Force Base in Denver, Colorado. Our paths separated at Lowery AFB, where he entered training much before I did. I was awaiting the security clearance necessary for the training school that took a while to complete. I believe that was because of the time I had spent in Oregon.

The trip from Lackland AFB in San Antonio, Texas to Lowery AFB in Denver, Colorado, was by railroad train, and it wasn't a bad trip at all. It took a day and a half, which meant we slept on the train in booths set up by porters. We traveled through the snowy mountains south of Denver before arriving just after dark on a cold and snowy day.

After being loaded onto buses, we were driven east along Colfax Avenue (part of U.S. Hwy 287) to the base. We were issued galoshes to were over our shoes as "snow boots." The first time I was "really cold" was after my arrival at Lowery.

After completing training at Lowery, I was assigned to Castle AFB in Merced, California. At the end of training in Denver, we were asked for our preferences for the next assignment locations. I had selected California, and Florida, I thought this was a good time to be in some glamorous (?) location and experience a different lifestyle.

While at Castle AFB, I completed, earlier than normal, the qualifications for an advanced skill level rating. I learned that the test was being administered in the near future and I thought I could advance myself by taking, and passing, that test, which I did. Only a few from my unit actually passed and I passed with a medial percentile score.

Shortly after attaining the rating, word came down of a program, created due to an overage in my career field, to reassign some of us with the advanced rating and cross-train to be instructors in a training school at Lowery AFB for aircraft weapons system maintenance and munitions loading on those aircraft. This was to assist the buildup of capabilities to meet the needs in Southeast Asia. I applied for the new assignment and was selected.

When at Castle AFB I enrolled in the local junior college and took classes held on the base and the downtown campus, in pursuit of a college degree. I took only two classes and completed them, but that was enough to complete an associate degree. With all the combination of courses I had taken I reckoned that the degree was in math and history, with some engineering courses added in. The actual degree wasn't awarded until the following June, but I was gratified that all the work I had done had finally resulted in a college degree – all of it financed from my own resources. While in Denver, I enrolled in the University of Colorado Denver Center and continued my pursuit of a full bachelor's degree. One course I took there that resonated with me was Sociology, which I found to be an almost "awakening" experience.

While in Denver I learned about an Air Force program to assist members to complete college degrees and become commissioned offers. All college and living expenses would be paid and the candidate would be given the rank of E-5, with all the benefits thereof. I took the officer and pilot qualification tests and passed them all with excellent percentile scores. I didn't pass the pervious GPA analysis. That was because of the 4-hour Spanish Course (mentioned previously) that I dropped after the half-semester. As I said previously, a military career may not have been the best selection for my personality.

I spent about two years at Lowery AFB before being assigned to the Tactical Air Force Command and ordered to Cannon AFB in eastern New Mexico (near Clovis). This was an additional training base for munitions loading crews and pilots. The pilots flew the F-100 Super Saber fighter/bomber aircraft. I had been there eight days, when orders came down for eight of us to be transitioned out to other bases and assignments: six were going to Viet Nam, one was going to Alaska, and I was going to Greece.

My assignment in Greece was to work as a NATO Safety Technical Monitor, which meant I would be watching the Greek Airmen load U.S. nuclear bombs on their F-104 Starfighter aircraft and seeing that it was done correctly and safely. I was stationed at near the city of Patras at an airbase called Araxos, which is on the Ionian Sea coastline of the Peloponnese region of Greece.

This was at a time when the country was still ruled by a king and a tour by the king was planned shortly after my arrival that would bring him by the military detachment housing where the living quarters were. Prior to the king's arrival the Greek villagers along the route had prepared large boughs of greenery over their houses and, ever spanning the roadway in some places; it was quite a spectacle.

On the appointed day, I went out to the main road where the king would be traveling. After a short while, the king and his queen came by in their open green Mercedes convertible, which he was driving. They were smiling and waving to the bystanders. This was, obviously, a time for celebration for the country. Later, in the month, an Army-led coup took place, overthrew the king and, eventually, exiled him from the country. My older brother, who was a Navy A-4 pilot at the time and in the Mediterranean Sea said preparations were made to enter the fight on behalf of the king, but that was never ordered. The military life for us at Araxos continued on, uninterrupted, as if nothing had happened.

The housing for our military detachment was located about a quarter mile off the Ionian Sea, which enabled us to spend a lot of time in, and on, the water. Waterskiing behind a runabout ski boat with its 50 horsepower Johnson outboard engine was available and I took advantage of it. I had, in Oregon, learned to ski, and to slalom ski, and, with this new opportunity, I became quite proficient at it. A French resort, we called "French Beach" was located several miles down the coastline. Several times I drove the boat over the sea to and from that resort. The trip got into some more open water than was around our beach and on one trip, waves, three to four feet high, were quartering the boat from behind. When one hit, I would try to negotiate it by revving the engine and running with the wave. The waves got a little higher and that strategy seemed not to work as well. The suggestion was made to turn right and go over the top of the wave. I tried that and it worked better, so we continued on.

At about mid-summer the City of Patras planned a Marina Festival. A retired Greek American and his wife had a summer residence there and a large cabin cruiser, which was anchored in the city harbor. It was proposed by this couple that our detachment personnel put on a waterskiing demonstration event to participate in the celebration. The cruiser came to our beach many times for us to assemble our team and to practice for the event. It was decided that one pass through the harbor be made with us four skiers in tow. The next pass was to be made with me on a slalom ski while all of the group was holding Greek and American flags.

The first pass was made without event, then, as we rounded the end of the pier, I tried to drop one ski and go slalom. This was something I had never practiced, and I lost my balance and fell into the water. I was picked up be a couple of men in a small boat who were laughing at my predicament and taken back to the area of the cruiser.

We decided to make another pass and prepared in the water to begin the run. This time I got up on the skis, but quickly decided to drop the one ski right then, at a slower speed, which is how I had always done it back at our beach. This worked well and the trips around the harbor and the flag display were successfully accomplished. It was reported that the crowd around the harbor enjoyed our display.

A write-up about the event appeared later in the "Stars and Stripes" U.S. Armed forces military newspaper in Europe that credited a Captain, who was along on the event, as being the manager and coordinator of the team – he had never before been involved until the actual event.

Later in the year, although the Greeks and the Turks were part of the NATO Alliance, the Turks overflew part of Greek airspace, apparently without the proper clearance. The Greek military went into a state of "full alert." For us that meant going into a full blackout state and being prepared to blow up our store of weapons. I spent two nights in the weapons storage area sleeping next to a nuclear weapon with a 40-pound shape charge sitting on it. For whatever reason, that, to me, wasn't as scary as it might sound.

When it came time to leave, I had gone through all the clearance procedures at the base and with the local police, but no one told me that I would be asked for documentation by a guard immediately before boarding the big TWA airplane that would take me back to the states. The customs agent/guard asked me, in broken English and Greek, for that paper, I was shocked and responded that I "Yes I had it, but it was in my luggage" which I had checked already and had no way to retrieve. Three times this was repeated by him, and I responded the same all three times. Finally, the guard waved me on, much to my relief.

The Boeing 707, with the big TWA letters on its tail and about 20 passengers aboard, finally took off and we were headed back to the states - via Rome, as it turned out. After landing in Rome, we were allowed off the plane and I strolled down the corridor to the terminal. After having done so, I thought I could say I had been in Italy.

We landed at JFK Airport in New York City, and I entered airport customs. An agent saw that I was a returning serviceman and welcomed me through. Later I took a prearranged limo ride to Fort Dix in New Jersey where I was processed out of the Air Force. I caught a midnight milk-run flight out of Philadelphia that made several stops, Baltimore and Nashville being two of those, and, finally, a smaller aircraft flight into Texarkana.

EPILOGUE

The pattern of abuse that my daddy had exhibited to me continued, I'm told, with my next two younger brothers. The one four years younger than me has stated that he had observed the interaction between my older brother, my daddy and me and had seen, as he put it, "The way he should go." It seems that worked for him, while the next one suffered much the same fate as I did, but not to the same degree. My mother has told me she intervened more to protect him than she ever dared to protect me.

Years later my daddy developed severe psychosis and was hospitalized for an extended time while receiving shock treatments. My mother told me he was a severe problem for the staff who said they had never seen anyone like him. Later, he was transferred to a veteran's hospital In Waco, Texas, where he was converted to oral drugs and subsequently released.

Later he developed a giant aneurism in his brain that was, in the main, inoperable. The aneurism blocked a duct from the brain gland the secreted spinal fluid and that caused a progressive build-up of pressure in the brain. The pressure was relieved by surgeons in Fort Worth who installed a tube in that brain area which emptied the fluid into his stomach. That seemed to work well, and he lived a retired life of fishing, camping, and playing golf.

I was able to live past the treatment I had received from him, and later enjoyed spending some time with him fishing and playing golf. I also, mischievously, enjoyed feeding his partiality to wine and would take him bottles of various blends which he mixed with Dr. Pepper before drinking.

Toward the end, he developed dementia and Alzheimer's Disease, and I was appointed as his guardian. I signed the papers that, according to his wishes, led to his death.

On the morning, he died, we were called to his bedside, but I was unavailable to immediately go there. As I was traveling later, I looked at the clock in my car and noted the time; it was 10:02 AM. I wished him a good journey and found out later It was the time he died.

www.ingramcontent.com/pod-product-compliance
Lightning Source LLC
Chambersburg PA
CBHW051141120626
46547CB00012B/904